Into the Clouds

Seeking Silver Linings

When I began to listen to poetry,
it's when I began to listen
to what clouds had to say,
and I began to listen to others.
And I think, most importantly for all of us,
then you begin to listen to the soul of yourself in here,
which is also the soul of everyone else.
Joy Harjo

Linda Varsell Smith

Thanks to

Maureen Frank: The Mandala Lady
for the preparing the manuscript for printing
and designing the covers and illustrations.

Court Smith: back cover photo

My poetry friends, critique groups.
intuitive consultants and family.

ISBN: 978-0-9888554-6-5

Rainbow Communications
471 NW Hemlock Ave.
Corvallis, OR 97330

varsell4@comcast.net

Linda Varsell Smith is a teacher, poet and novelist
who lives in Corvallis, Oregon with her husband Court
in a mini-museum of her miniature collections
of Swedish folk art, angels, winged beings and seasonal collections.
She taught creative writing, children's literature and literary publication
at Linn-Benton Community College.
She teaches Write Your Life Story and poetry workshops.
Linda was an editor for Calyx Books for 32 years
and LBCC's The Eloquent Umbrella, literary magazine.
Former president of the Oregon Poetry Association,
current president of Portland PEN Women .
she belongs to several writing groups as well as
plays competitive and cooperative Scrabble.
A great fan of dance, gymnastics, plays and art.

Table of Contents
From a little spark may burst a flame. Dante Alighieri

Head in the Clouds
Being Multidimensional

Cloud of Unknowing
Cloudlets of Creative Interpretations

Beneath the Clouds
On the Witness Stand

Cloud-Gathering
2016 Elections

Clouded Mind
Moodlings

Beclouded
Attempts at Healing

Cloudscapes
Quirks

Cloudy Weather
Climate Changes

Cloudbursts
Global Gleanings

Lost in the Clouds
Ancient Discoveries

In the "Cloud"
Dealing with Technology

Beyond Clouds
Exploring the Cosmos

Head in the Clouds

Being Multidimensional

Poetry that sustains me is when I feel
that for a minute,
the clouds have parted
and I've seen
ecstasy or something.
Rita Dove

River in the Sky

River in the sky is what I call the milky way.
Oh to be a flying light with wings to go anywhere.   Serena Supplee

Why just the Milky Way river? As flying light
I hope to explore other galaxies and universes.
So many spaces to shine a flashlight.
I believe in the plurality of worlds- multiverses.
> We are starstuff from stardust.
> In the cosmos, can I trust?

I hope to explore other galaxies and universes,
with dimensions, sentience, fascinating beings.
Light matter and dark matter, energy rehearses
the dances of life with diverse decreeings.
> Many universes with many gods,
> planning genesis, sending out squads.

So many spaces to send a flashlight.
We are starry sparks- cosmic discoverers.
Our higher essence is quite bright.
Our mission to be love-uncoverers.
> We were meant to shine--.
> each a potential golden mine.

I believe in the plurality of worlds–multiverses.
I sense I have lived in many space-scapes,
not all on this green rock from this sun–my verses
extol Earth's seascapes, skyscapes, landscapes,
> but in my dreams and imagination
> I leave my body to another destination.

We are starstuff from stardust
starseeded for this earthly experience.
Looking for meaning, appears a must
with every inkling and intelligence.
> I hope any rivers in the sky
> continue to flow and don't run dry.

In the cosmos, can I trust
the journey has a purpose, some resolution?
Will my starlight burn out, blast or bust?
Do I subconsciously know the solution?
> Sink or swim, dim or shine
> Starry stuff probably is divine.

Tripping the Light Fantastic

Living in the etheric realm.,.creates a chasm when you with your peaceful, serene heart, with your beautiful connection to the world of spirit light, attempt to make casual conversation with someone who doesn't speak your language.
Sara Wiseman

Apparently some Earthlings spend a lot of time
in the etheric realm communing with the Divine.
Ways some folks do this is by meditating, prayer
contemplation and nature. They have a lot of alone time.
If you live in the etheric, you live in a different vibration
than many people around you.

These etheric folk live in a state of peace
quiet and calm while the world
rages around in chaos and drama.
The rest of us live the distracted life,
indulge in superficial endeavors,
shallow conversations, mundane concerns.

Wouldn't it be fun to trip the light fantastic,
live in the etheric, existing in a different dimension
while still living this grounded earth life?
These spiritual beings find some things
just do not matter that much anymore.
They have moved on to a new place of understanding.

If you get to this etheric place, you relax,
step into your true purpose. (Maybe dance?)
Be what you're here to be. (Wouldn't that be nice to know?)
Many of us are here to be light weight lifters.
When we lift ourselves up to new understanding
we begin to lift the world. Pretty amazing.

If I get to trip the light fantastic in the etheric realm,
if I am to perform my purpose, I'd need to at least
tiptoe on the earthly plane. Earth's heaviness and darkness
needs lightening. From whatever dimension I get ideas,
I would like to perform lightsomely—not detached or alone
but connected—together light-lifting to the stars.

Roaming Many Worlds

*Every philosophy and every psychological system has been based upon inadequate
knowledge of certain aspects of existence, upon a partial insight. We need a greater
experience, a multidimensional metaphysics. Now as ever before, we are capable of it.
We can learn from all the traditions, from both their strengths and weaknesses. But to
do this we must roam these many worlds, high and low.*   Michael Murphy

In our quest for knowing and meaning
we explore many systems: spirituality, science,
philosophy, psychology, math, art, gleaning
insight into what is going on. Are we in compliance?
> Do we accept or reject suggestions?
> Create new or review old expressions?

We explore many systems: spirituality, science
to figure out what consists of our constitution.
Are we controlled or do we have self-reliance?
Will our questions be answered, find resolution?
> Is truth in anything infallible, eternal?
> Are we ever to get beyond the kernel?

Philosophy, psychology, math, art gleaning
with their own methods add to the brew.
Inputs to existence's purpose convening?
Creativity needed to see ideas through.
> If there are nine dimensions and most of us in 3D--
> are above and below dimensions open to humanity?

Insight into what is going on, are we in compliance?
Do some people know? Illuminati, alien networks any security?
The Council of Nine, World Management Team, faiths dance?
Renegades, Galactic Federation? Prime Creator committee?
> Where comes the help to understand clearly?
> I want to sense All and not see blearily.

Do we accept or reject suggestions?
Do we really have angels, spirits and guides?
Are we multidimensional? Capable of progressions?
Can we get beyond duality and embrace all sides?
> All is consciousness and energy some say.
> What are our challenges and blockages on our way?

Create new or review old expressions?
Bloom from the codes and imprints inside us?
Stretch to the sky, find peace in concessions?
When we leave this dimension is anyone beside us?
> In dreams, life regressions we roam other places.
> Our eternal soul, entities belong in many spaces?

Creating a New Cosmic Citizen?

Just why are we tinkering with the human race?
Is it to make us healthier and stronger?
Hybrids, robots, androids, cyborgs to explore space?
So we are not bio-based any longer?
       Transhumans left with no original parts?
       Carbon ends and silicon starts?

Is it just to make us healthier and stronger?
What about smarter, more strands of DNA?
Changes to become an outerspace-monger
in case Earth doesn't want us to stay?
       Will consciousness fit on a chip?
       What dysfunctions can we strip?

Hybrids, robots, androids, cyborgs to explore space?
Will they share with fleshy forms ground time?
Will our intelligence keep pace?
What priorities will be prime?
       Can all forms live together?
       Who actually controls the tether?

So we are not bio-based any longer?
Created by 3-D printer, assembly line, incubator?
Who is thinking of Gaia? Prolong her
suffering while we push the high-tech accelerator
       to leave her in our unsustainable trash?
       Perhaps we'll become asteroidal ash.

Transhumans left with no original parts--
physical or non-tech thought?
Creating future fleshy cosmic ooparts?
What meaning has our existence brought?
       Are we guided by alien kin
       trying to get under our skin?

Carbon ends and silicon starts?
Does it matter what we are made of?
We are formless when our life force departs.
What matters most? Eternal life? Love?
       Whatever is in store for earthly folks
       will the intention be harmonic strokes?

Choreographing A Dancing Star
You need chaos in your soul to give birth to a dancing star. Friedrich Nietzsche

A positive use for chaos in my soul.
I have tried many steps to understand.
What is my earthy- cosmic role?
Dancing thoughts are not under my command.
       Release light for a dancing star?
       I'd create this universe more stellular.

I have tried many steps to understand
life's meaning, create patterns, cracks for light--
hoping for clarity, creativity to expand.
To birth intense light, one needs insight.
       My eyes can see stars in the sky,
       but not within me, I wonder why?

What is my earthly-cosmic role?
To be teacher, dancer, writer, singer?
Am I linked to a multiversal goal?
As systems-buster? A light-bringer?
       Dance is everywhere- a boomerang
       to come to us, to ignite interabang.

Dancing thoughts are not under my command.
They remain within. My body can't manifest
my choreographic dream. I witness wonderland
of other dancers realizing their quest.
       My soul does retain chaos, ready to birth
       any dancing light from darkened Earth.

Release light for a dancing star!
Get through all the humbuggery.
Stage an enlightened avatar.
Shed all the baggage and drudgery.
       Oh, to be so splendiferous, celestial,
       to dance lightsomely beyond terrestrial!

I'd create this universe more stellular
yet despite all my efforts my soul spirals, spins.
I'd love to give star-dancing a try
but my attempts seem widdershins.
       Still the idea this dancing star could exist,
       is a challenge I find impossible to resist.

Cloud-Chaser

Dancing through the clouds of unknowing
exploring transmutations of the sky-scape,
discovering densities and contours showing
constant change, finding new thoughts to shape.
>Another idea or theory to ponder.
>I am immersed in wonder.

Exploring transmutations of the sky-scape
imprinting concepts that resonate.
Certain impressions I can't escape,
compel me to contemplate.
>I am a cloud-chaser for clear thought.
>I want to remain free, not caught.

Discovering densities and contours showing
many dimensions and many sources,
I partner for various durations knowing
I might find higher resources.
>A cloud-chaser is in a cosmic race.
>A cloud-chaser can also avoid or erase.

Constant change, finding new thoughts to shape
keeps me evaluating, a follower of no one.
Aspects of many illuminations leave me agape
but each of us is unique with our souls undone.
>A cloud-chaser tries to clarify a cloudy mind.
>Each cloud-chaser has an ensouled self to find.

Another idea or theory to ponder
keeps me exited to find new light.
I'm a clouded receiver and responder
awaiting the rainbow, lightning, sprite.
>Perhaps a cloud whose droplets don't land
>in my earnest attempts to understand.

I am immersed in wonder
floating through consciousness energy.
Peering into clouds, not a magic-wander
looking for places of synergy.
>Juggling particles of existence,
>a cloud-chaser with persistence.

Nibbling Breadcrumbs

> *Life is meant to be a mystery. Life can't be anything more than a great, vast, unknown. We are never given the whole map, that would be dull. We are given the next breadcrumb on our path.* Sara Wiseman

Nibbling breadcrumbs is not very nourishing.
I yearn for a whole, healthy loaf of my choice.
I want a life that's not dull, but flourishing.
I desire ways to express my voice.
        Is each individual path a quagmire?
        Too much effort for each trier?

I yearn for a whole, healthy loaf of my choice
with a dark chocolate dessert.
Who delivers the invoice?
How much energy must I exert?
        I am getting old, tired and achy.
        My less nimble choices-- rather shaky.

I want a life that's not dull, but flourishing,
filled with love and imagination.
I want limbs and ideas swishing,
seeking my next surprising destination.
        I am not fond of murder mystery plots
        or unknowns not filed in their slots.

I desire ways to express my voice,
to glean information multidimensionally,
discover experiences to rejoice,
live authentically and intentionally,
        despite no maps or GPS for assistance,
        to guide my uniquely personal existence.

Is each individual path a quagmire?
Any respites on the way?
Was there a pre-birth chart prior
to provide purpose, skills in my DNA?
        What essence plans all these unknowable things--
        all the love, challenges and sufferings?

Too much effort for each trier?
Earth has some heavy, cruel ground rules.
I am a reluctant earthly resident buyer--
a non-violent rebel without adequate tools.
        I pursue my best despite this plight
        to chase darkness, bring light.

Re-Choosing Reality

Try this out. Let go of everything around you. Let go of everything in you. Let go of the body.
Let go of time. Just hang out in Noplace. No time. Aaah...what a treat! Miriam Dyak

If I could start from scratch
from just a figment of my imagination,
what manifestations would I hatch?
What would be new my creation?
       Would I have the tools of a Divine Mind?
       What assistance would I find?

From just a figment of my imagination
how would I fill this vast void?
What would I bring into realization?
What challenges would I avoid?
       If I could, I'd bring back light,
       turn blue the color of night.

What manifestations would I hatch?
Dimensions with various densities?
Sentient beings I could match
to harmonic, curious diversities?
       I would insist on one rule.
       Be kind and never cruel.

What would be new in my creation?
I'd start small and expand gradually,
experiment with consciousness and sensation
for a peaceful existence at least initially.
       I am not sure what I'd have to work with:
       choices, sacred geometry, energy, labyrinth?

Would I have the tools of a Divine Mind?
Is this coup just a temporary take-over?
Would my cosmic changes bind
universal progress by an inept make-over?
       This incarnation is hard enough.
       To be responsible for All–too tough.

What assistance would I find?
Why would it all depend on me?
This order I'd rescind.
Might join a life-sustaining committee.
       Perhaps, fortunately, I'll not have the chance
       or duty to cosmically alter and enhance.

Idiosyncrasy

Why do you never find anything written about that idiosyncratic thought you avert to, about your fascination with something no one else understands? Because it is up to you.
Annie Dillard

I admit to being idiosyncratic.
It's part of my curiosity.
I am progressively democratic,
with quirky creativity.
      I figure others do understand
      things not currently in my command.

It's part of my curiosity
to explore the cosmos, oddities.
to puncture people's pomposity,
to collect miniature commodities.
      I let my imagination roam.
      I'm multidimensionally at home.

I am progressively democratic
fantastical and quizzical in thought.
Scientific discoveries are mathematic
and not the only knowledge I've sought.
      I don't seem to have the need
      to commit to any institutional creed.

With quirky curiosity
I seek to learn from many places,
new ideas, possibilities with diversity,
try to avoid violent dark spaces.
      I want to know life's meaning, to do
      what I came for and to follow through.

I figure others do understand.
I am not alone in my wonderings.
I'm a Pleiadian in fairyland.
I enjoy playful ponderings.
      I 'm symptomatically iconoclastic.
      I relish being somewhat eccentric.

Things not currently in my command
might not ever be.
Some things are unknown and banned
I accept full responsibility
      for my beliefs and actions–
      others' unsympathetic reactions.

Dimensional Discoveries

Why am I exploring other dimensional theories
when I don't comprehend 3D duality?
The Pleiadian perspective explains nine inquiries.
I have a long way to go, apparently.
> For the Earth-centric prone
> this indicates we are not alone.

When I don't comprehend 3D duality
what makes me think I'll understand other D's better?
1D is Earth's center iron core crystal to see
it holds Akashic records to the letter.
> 2D between crystal and the crust forces--
> magma, telluric realm, volcanic resources.

The Pleiadian perspective explains nine inquiries.
Most Earthlings are dwelling in 3D.
Place of linear space and time familiarities,
with karma and duality.
> 4D is collective mind of our thought and feeling--
> realm of global control patterns to keep us reeling.

I have a long way to go, apparently
I'd like to bypass 4D's sun body canopy.
I'd like to raise to 5D frequency--
unconditional love, open heart panoply
> Must overcome duality, 4D to access.
> Must seek ways to progress.

For the Earth-centric prone
6D world of forms and sacred geometry,
crop circles thrill me to the bone,
yet remain a elusive mystery.
> 7D deals with sound. 8D divine mind
> and consciousness. Hard to find.

This indicates we are not alone
9D is Mayan time codes for evolution
for everything that exists. A calendar of our own
for our alchemical transmutation.
> A cosmic citizen of this universe
> connected to an expanding multiverse.

Nine Dimensions

The lower dimensions (1D and 2D) are various levels of Earth (3D)–from core to surface; the fourth dimension (4D) is the realm of collective thought that bridged the physical and unseen worlds; and the fifth through ninth dimensions (5D-9D) are celestial. Barbara Hand Clow

The nine dimensions ground in the center of Earth.
They extend into the Galactic Center.
Western spirituality find first four of great worth.
Higher ones Eastern mysticism enter.
      Math takes some scientists beyond 4D
      It all sounds very magical to me.

They extend into the Galactic Center
on a vertical axis, various consciousness in charge.
Each level has its own presenter
and helps our multi-dimensionality enlarge.
      Iron Core Earth Crystal anchors 1D
      10D headed by Andromeda Galaxy.

Western spirituality find the first four of great worth.
Humanity is in charge of Linear Space and Time-3D.
New Agers are seeking a 5D berth
away from collective 4D mind of Annunaki.
      5D is love and creativity
      guided by the Pleiades.

Higher ones Eastern mysticism enter.
6D is Morphic fields, Sacred Geometry.
Sirius helps to re-center.
Galactic Informational Highways of Light in 7D
      lead by Andromeda Galaxy.
      Cosmic Order/ Galactic Federation-Orion 8D

Math takes some scientists beyond 4D
far from Milky Way Galactic Center 9D with Tzolk'in.
Will we ever reach 9D? More D's?
When will we meet all these cosmic kin?
      Pleiadeans gave Clow this information.
      In me it struck a resonating vibration.

It all sounds very magical to me.
The complexity is google-plex immense.
Though I can't comprehend its entirety,
I believe innately it does make sense.
      I believe the matrix is intentional
      Earthlings are multi-dimensional.

Climbing the Vertical Axis

The lower dimensions (1D and 2D) are various levels of Earth (3)–from the core to surface; the fourth dimension (4D) is the realm of collective thought that bridges the physical and unseen worlds and the fifth-ninth (5D -9 D) are celestial...Culturally the first four dimensions correspond somewhat to Western spirituality and the higher ones to Eastern mysticism....since the eighth dimension (8D) teaches how to live impeccably in the material world and 8D teaching motivated them, it was initially outrageous to imagine that the dimensions influenced by distant star systems–the Pleiades in the fifth dimension (5D), Sirius in the sixth dimension (6D);Andromeda in the seventh dimension (7D); Orion in the 8th dimension (8D) and the Milky Way in the ninth dimension (9D)–can actually influence us here on Earth. Perhaps this is why our ancestors believed the stars had consciousness and were repositories of their stories and myths. Barbara Hand Clow

Our ancestors passed on many stories and myths
about celestial encounters and otherworldly beings.
Spirituality and science are beginning to look closer
into ancient wisdom to help us understand our present.

4D is the zone where we can access higher-frequency visions.
We are wired to higher dimensions through images
time-released from the Galactic Center
through active intuition and intense feelings.

Clow suggests we can locate our personal pathways
in the great landscape of cosmic potential
by feeling our way in the fourth dimension
and clearing our heads of junk images.

She suggests we live in a media-soaked 4D zone
where most people can't see the portal doors to higher worlds.
We need to awaken to reconstruct and clear the 4D zone
to identify the vibrational frequencies of all nine dimensions.

We can heal ourselves and the planet, if we tune in
and understand these dimensions and how they work.
I love her concepts on crop circles and sacred geometry.
Her interpretations of the Mayan calendar inspire me.

I am exploring her concepts and techniques
as I want to climb the vertical axis of consciousness.
What dimension am I in when I dream?
What dimension will my soul go to when I die?

I'd like to de-clutter 4D. Utilize the best of the first 4 D's
Some talk of a 5th dimensional shift. Higher vibes.
Newcomers' DNA tweaked to uplift codes for living
with a higher frequency. They can help save the unawakened.

My research fascinates me. The Matrix, energy fields,
everything having energy and consciousness.
In an Age of Extremes in the Anthropocene.
We need to change our mindset.

Old ways have brought much destruction.
New ways bring hope for connections
that could usher in a more peaceful,
cooperative and sustainable world.

I accept I will never have all the answers
to my questions. I question my free will,
bodily equipment, my ability to ask the right questions.
I seek resonances for my soul.

Every once in a while I will read or see something,
feel internal music to uplift my spirits.
In the midst of chaos, I gather calm.
I know I am but one soul-splinter connected to the cosmos.

I only know what I have consciously received.
I do not know where my night dreams take me.
I hear I am multidimensional.
Do I face the same conundrums there?

My head-heart brains seem constructed
to ponder and express only what I can grasp.
I want to spiral up the vertical axis
and take a peek as to what is possible.

Decoding DNA

I wonder how they counted over 50 trillion cells
in our body with the center of cells double helix strands
with nucleotides, each strand six feet long,
62 billion miles long if added them all--,
Earth to sun 300 times.
Wow are we full of it?

DNA has three molecules and four bases.
It is the blueprint to tell cells what to do.
All living things have all this assistance.
2% are genes and 98% once considered junk DNA.
But that 98% regulates the body's activity.
Wow are we full of it?

DNA mirrors our environment,
responds to what we think, say or do.
DNA holds soul travels,
maps for cellular response.
We can access healing light.
Wow are we full of it?

There are attunement processes
and sacred transmissions of energy.
We can change our vibration.
We can integrate and increase energy,
receive messages of healing and wisdom.
Wow are we full of it?

Multidimensional awareness and connection.
Transmute with pillars of light.
Achieve high vibe energy frequencies
into an energetic blueprint, part of our light-body
grid of mother Earth and electromagnetic Earth.
Wow are we full of it?

All this power and energy surrounds us.
We can bring deeper awareness making
this easier to practice? Surpass the ordinary.
Beyond the limitations of the material universe.
Heal from physical and mental illness.
Wow are we full of it?

If we can tap the power of our DNA
we can improve decision making, function stronger,
become a planetary light-worker--
a better being of love and light.
Some say this miracle is possible.
Wow are we full of it?

I would like to study DNA activation and attunement,
explore Angel and crystal healing therapy, hypnotherapy,
past life regression, Usui Reiki, spiritual and chakra healing–
ways to elevate my consciousness, increase light.
All these DNA strands wait for us to maximize them.
Just think- wow we are full of it!

Becoming Radial?

There is talk of altering our DNA
to make us enhanced human beings.
Maybe become hybrids or robots some day.
All kinds of possibilities they're seeing.
   Maybe we won't be carbon-based.
   Will we be bi-laterally encased?

To make us enhanced human beings-
smarter, sturdier, disease-free,
new advances-scientific decreeings
make extreme alterations a possibility.
   Change contents in our baggage,
   could we reduce the carnage?

Maybe become hybrids or robots some day.
We could become an interplanetary breed,
to populate places, spaced far, far, away.
Will we tinker to find what we need?
   Will consciousness follow form?
   What could be our next cosmic uniform?

All kinds of possibilities they're seeing.
All these parts exchanges, new designs.
With many limitations gone, could be freeing.
I'm dreaming along sea star lines.
   Radial symmetry gives panoramic views,
   no blood, sexual fluidity holds new clues.

Maybe we won't be carbon-based.
We could build beings with different star stuff.
Our fragile bio-beings might be erased.
Are we just not adaptable enough?
   Sea stars have armor, replace whole from one limb
   Asteroidia have arm-tip eyes, suction-cups to climb.

Will we be bi-laterally encased?
I like vibrant color, radial symmetry.
Our inherent flaws have re-surfaced?
Will we explore other sacred geometry?
   Perhaps a re-vamped sea star, radiant rays like sun?
   Keen eyes on multi-tasking limbs mean more hugs for everyone?

Cloud Nine

I wonder why euphoria is on cloud nine.
They say there are eleven dimensions.
Is the experience so divine
it's beyond my intentions?
        Cloud nine must be very elevated,
        it's so longed for and celebrated.

They say there are eleven dimensions.
Does cloud nine float within minds and hearts?
Does each dimension have joyous extensions?
How do we find its component parts?
        Cloud nine experience sounds so special.
        I hope it does not remain celestial.

Is the experience so divine
only some people feel its power?
Even clouded folks seek nine's design
to bring glowing rays lower.
        Clouds come in many shapes,
        create many moods and mind-scapes.

It's beyond my intentions?
It remains in metaphor?
Among other Earthling inventions
to guess what we're here for?
        Does cloud nine illumination come from above
        or any time we generate kindness or love?

Cloud nine must be very elevated
as revealed in poetry and song.
For most, happiness is being elated
with hope to keep us moving along.
        Cloud Nine is like a beacon light
        to guide our way in our darkest night.

It's so longed for and celebrated
because it uplifts our lives on Earth.
We yearn to be illuminated
to find harmony and worth.
        Cloud Nine might be a wispy dream--
        the cloud with a silver lining seam.

Delving into Dreams

No matter what people tell you, words and ideas can change the world. Robin Williams

In another place, in a different time,
more youthful Robin Williams and I met
with a group of educators at a conference.

Robin was a professor at Columbia
revolutionizing English instruction.
He offered to mentor me for a Masters degree.

I was teaching at a community college
on the west coast, balancing
family and part-time teaching.

As my husband entertained
our three young children,
I revived my dream.

I planned to spend a semester on campus,
skype, work on- line with Robin.
I was ecstatic at the opportunity.

When I was about to enter college at 18,
my parents could not afford Columbia
and did not want me in New York.

I left behind my high school sweetheart,
went to a local state college and met
my new boyfriend studying in New York.

In an alternative reality perhaps
I went to Columbia, and Robin was a teacher--
perhaps lived our first choices for our goals.

Though I did get a Masters in Educational Psychology
I was not allowed to teach creative writing full-time
or basic English courses without a Masters in English.

In this current reality I did get to teach courses I loved,
but never even visited Columbia. But in this dream,
I was able to fulfill long-suppressed desires.

Perhaps Robin and I live in a dimension
where dreams do come true,
not where dreams are deferred or died.

You're only given a little spark of madness. You mustn't lose it. Robin Williams

Haunting

On a night surreal journey
I peer out a window and see
gray cloudy-like figures
dancing on a ridge
against a vivid, red-orange sunset.

The figures are smudges,
the shade of rain-clouds
with no distinguishable features.
Pale shadows gleefully, ghostly dancing.
Back-lighted. I am youthful too.

Somehow I cross the street
and look out another window.
A friend and I gaze upon a rocky beach
and comment we are in the home
and see the sea someone else saw.

There are twin beds. We decide to sleep.
I awake screaming. Some unseen energy
tugs at my legs. I struggle to kick free.
I go to the other side of the room and shout
for the energy to leave for the rest of my life.

I tell my friend that was my first haunting.
The room teems with large, black, stinging ants.
As we leave, we feel the energy pull at us.
We huddle near a parked car to block the force.
then scramble to the house across the street.

My friend and I talk about the strange encounter.
There is a mirror which she looks into, not me.
A naked, young, adolescent blonde girl walks
out of a bathroom and wordlessly passes us by.
I wake with a leg cramp, wondering where I have been.

Before I go to sleep I ask for dreams
to give clear understandings I can share.
Well, I am sharing this dream with no clear
understanding of the full meaning except
I do not like dark energies invading my space.

Invisible Worlds

Dimensions
beyond our vision
have beings,
consciousness.
Not seeing, yet believing
we are not alone.

Stardust clumps
into matter, gloms
physical forms,
yet star stuff
can be different from us
elsewhere in vast space.

Matter with
possibilities
filled with life
amazes.
Sacred geometry for
experiences.

We don't know
all the cosmic plans.
Universe
only one
of multiple universes.
Beyond brain-boggling.

Sharing a Message

Without sharing there can be no justice;
Without justice there can be no peace.
Without peace, there can be no future.
Maitreya

A group called The Masters headed by Maitreya
a World Teacher, not a religious leader,
but an educator will inspire us to create
a new civilization – Golden Age?

We are to imagine a world free of war,
poverty and injustice–where sharing
and cooperation have replaced
greed and competition.

Other pundits of hope purvey
a similar message with similar goals,
various methods of delivery–
to a deeply traumatized populace.

Maitreya says change can come
with extraordinary, wise, incorruptible
leadership– working with women
and men of goodwill around the world.

With current global leadership?
Where are the bright stars?
A world leader like the USA needs
to dump Trump, not pillory Hillary.

This time love, wisdom and compassion
would come from advanced enlightened souls
who will return to public roles in the world–
with advice :"Share and save the world".

Sounds like a cosmic bailout
and Masters of Wisdom sounds
like another male hierarchy.
Billions more people to save this time.

Apparently this Spiritual Hierarchy
are custodian of energies entering the Earth
to fulfill Earth's Divine Plan: The Plan of Evolution--
another of humanity's Eldest Brothers.

This literature uses term man for all genders.
Maitreya is another crisis teacher like
Krishna, Buddha, Confucius, Jesus, Mohammed–
we are in a deep mess—why not send a woman?

They say the Masters won't infringe on free will.
Maitreya is emerging gradually and we need
to take steps toward unity and co-operation.
Eventually they will help us overcome global crises.

A Golden Age will address mass poverty,
ecological collapse, endless war. We will build
an era of world brotherhood (need better term)
This movement needs to upgrade language.

All the promised enhancing of the Earth grid,
raising frequencies and vibrations,
creating the fifth dimension and New Earth
requires otherworldly assistance.

Mention of Ageless and Ancient Wisdom,
cosmically sent teachers and saviors
sounds heavenly and utopian–but so far
not enough Earthlings are listening.

These messengers seem pie in the sky.
There is an upper crust and a bottom crust.
What is the filling? Does each individual
get an equal slice of the pie?

Igniting the Spark

We are here. We come to put a spark of remembrance in you.
Pleiadian message.

Humans, a fragment of spirit,
we intuit.

Enlivened part of creation--
incarnation.

Spirit eternal, wisdom light
is to enlight.

Will we gain the hoped for insight?
Wherever people had their start,
what did we come here to impart?
We intuit, incarnation is to enlight?

Being Multidimensional

Seem to spend most time in 3D–
       puzzle to me.

Higher, lighter dimensions lure–
       strongly allure

to realms of E.T. entities,
       to Pleiades.

I speculate realities
in this form, but don't know of
all possibilities above
puzzle to me. Strongly allure to Pleiades.

Expanding My Cloud of Unknowing

For decades I felt I failed my son, Kip.
I was told he had died so I would grow spiritually—
just at the time I felt god-forsaken.

With no organized faith to sustain me,
I floundered through contacts and books
exploring my path through the cloud of unknowing.

I discovered spirituality, not religion,
but I did not want anyone to die, so
I would grow—especially not a beloved son.

This heavy burden kept me from recovery.
If I did not grow, he had died in vain?
How would I know if I succeeded?

For awhile I'd leave my body during sleep.
Kip would tell me what to look into. I'd research
the fragments of what I remembered upon waking.

Once during an activation, he came from Aldebaron
to energize his ailing mother through a healer.
He came to heal my wounded body and spirit.

Another time an intuitive said he was now
a source of light darting across the cosmos.
Our starships passed in another dimension.

During a past-life regression about 1900
we were mother and son. He died tragically young.
I crumbled. This life a chance to handle death better.

Still, I felt I failed my son this time around.
What if I couldn't fulfill his expectation?
What if I can't realize my mission?

Finally a shaman heard Kip say,
"Mom, I came in for my own destiny. I love you
and want to thank you for allowing me to come in."

He said I had it all wrong.
I was not living to grow for him.
He came in for himself. I had my own goals.

Why did it take decades to tell me?
It took someone who could hear him?
Burden lifted. I can celebrate his life unclouded.

The latest transmission relayed Kip came for data.
He was on reconnaissance to collect my energetic
signature to find me anywhere in the cosmos.

We are not working together
in this dimension now—
but in another dimension.

Finally I am comforted, connected to a beloved
spirit in many manifestations. I rejoice
in the gathering cumulous cloud of unknowing.

Cloud of Unknowing

Cloudlets of Creative Interpretations

Do you wish to rise?
Begin by descending.
You plan a tower
that will pierce the clouds?
Lay first the foundation
of humility.

Saint Augustine

Mining Silver Linings

Clouds appear to have a silver lining
but don't some seem to glow gold?
When we are in our thought-mining,
go for the gold, I've been told.
       Silver linings reveal edge of sun,
       signify better times or situation.

But don't some seem to glow gold,
rimmed with sunlight promising sunrise?
Maybe golden opportunities will unfold.
Silver might be a compromise.
       Silver and gold rays emanate from within?
       Clouds reveal new expressions might begin?

When we are in our thought-mining,
looking inside and out.
We gaze at clouds, land's undermining
our lofty intentions. We doubt.
       Silver and gold are colorful concepts
       lining what our sentience accepts.

Go for gold, I've been told.
but I am not seeking the status of winning.
A rainbow-- unranked, I behold...
my challenges are just beginning.
       I don't need a medal of gold or silver.
       I am just a questing soul-sliver.

Silver linings reveal edge of sun--
light lurking ready to shine forth.
A new mindset could have begun,
could glow golden henceforth.
       Clouds color-change, have no number,
       shape-shift, disencumber.

Signify better times or situation?
Do clouds provide any benefit?
Is this hope pure imagination?
What can a cloud transmit?
       For me clouds can be off-duty
       and just provide water and beauty.

Awakening

Awakening is the new spiritual buzz word.
Consciousness raising is the goal.
Collective consciousness is what's heard.
We need to dig deep to become whole.
        Try to be non-judgmental, uplift.
        Yoga and meditation center the drift.

Higher consciousness raising is the goal.
We seek a higher vibration.
Can we create a diamond out of coal
in any problematic situation?
        Challenges are part of life's journey
        until laid out dead on a Gurney?

Collective conscious is what's heard
on media, from hierarchal institutions.
Negativity in news, dogma inferred.
We could make better resolutions.
        We might strive for creativity and love,
        give violence, suffering, conflict a shove.

We need to dig deep to become whole.
Align with the present and "isness" of things?
We've watched dysfunction take its toll.
Wonder what awakening brings?.
        A multi-traumatized species knows pain.
        Can we transcend to light once again?

Try to be non-judgmental and uplift.
Awakening is very hard to do.
How do we make this frequency shift?
Can we make a universal breakthrough?
        Can we take down masks, reconstruct ego?
        Can we become authentic? Just let go?

Yoga and meditation center the drift
as the world swirls around us. But when
exploring within, will we find light gift?
Can we awaken enough spiritual specimen?
        We can't consciously cocoon
        and expect awakening will come soon.

The Third Eye

The third eye (also known as the inner eye) is a mystical and esoteric concept referring to a speculative invisible eye which provides perception beyond ordinary sight. Wikipedia

Lots of concepts of the Third Eye.
Perhaps all are myth or hoax?
I love the ideas. I want to try
to see what third eye can coax.
From Hinduism, Chan, Taoism or theosophy?
From Buddhism, Christianity, New Age spirituality?

Perhaps all are myth or hoax
but connection to cosmos is appealing.
Strongly supported by speculative folks,
enhanced functions they're revealing--
enlightenment, visions, precognition,
chakras, auras, out-of-body conditions.

I love the ideas. I want to try
inner realms, inner consciousness spaces.
With the pineal gland will I spy
some of these surreal, cosmic places?
Some third eye users are called seers.
Others claim atrophied gland is in arrears.

To see what third eye can coax
would involve training and specialists who
correct vibration to the universe, strokes
to open third eye by techniques to follow through.
Some claim to develop sight: microscopic
and etheric tube vision that is telescopic.

From Hinduism, Chan ,Taoism or Theosophy,
Third Eye above eyebrow or middle of forehead,
or reduced ancient pineal gland in another philosophy.
Taoism says in sixth chakra, of main meridian instead,
in Upper Dan Tien (upper cinnabar field) or
"muddy pellet" from their energy centers' core.

From Buddhism, Christianity, New Age Spirituality--
Christians say third eye relates to non-dualistic thinking.
Theosophists relate to circadian rhythms of light polarity.
But many think pineal gland dormant or shrinking.
Goal to understand reality: unsatisfactory, impermanent
and unsubstantial? Clear the vision of this "divine eye"?

Good Versus Evil Decision

I am an advocate for good.
Be angelic as we should.
Live in peace, harmony and light.
Relish doing happy things right.

Be in league with angels and saints.
Reject violence and what taints.
Believe in hope, pie-in-the-sky.
Expect disappointment, but try

Or consider

I am an advocate for evil.
Be a satanistic devil.
Live with spice, drugged out pleasure.
Be narcissistic–in full measure.

Fight in wars or mingle with thieves.
Learn what liar and cheater receives.
Be free to do what you want to so
you can expect hell when you go?

Oh God!

Good gawd?   Flawed God?
God to question? God to laud?
        God that is divine and perfect?
        God that operates with defect?
Which concept of God do you follow?
What connection will you allow?

If we are a God soul-splinter-
God motivated soul-sprinter
        who set this energy in motion
        causing a cosmic commotion?
Are we just an experiment
in ways souls are sentient?

If our belief thinks God is good
and there are rituals and rules we should
        guide our lives by, worship higher-beings--
        are we experiencing the best we're seeing?
Are good and evil our only choice?
Choose right and you'll rejoice?

But if you believe in a flawed God
who passed imperfections to us seems odd,
        while the universal creator is still testing
        and various quests are contesting--
is the multiverse still in process?
Will we contribute to its success?

Some people don't believe God exists,
yet some creative energy persists
        to cause generative, decisive, divisive acts,
        battling evil, truths, theories and ALL facts.
God as innovator, scientist, confused deist?
God as programmer, tinkerer, elusive theorist?

God to pray to?   God to swear to?
God to petition to? God to compare to?
        Is the Prime Creator of ALL
        at our beck and call?
God who sends earthly teachers?
Or are each of us cosmic outreachers?

Counting on God—are there many?
Or life's just some fluke and there aren't any?
        I'd like a God of hope, peace and love,
        making me safe, below, inside, above.
I have no idea how to envision a pure energy God,
genderless, invisible, all-powerful with no spiritual prod.

Am I a spark from the Great Sparkler?
From a luminous enlightener or snuffing darkler?
        Am I an omniversal ort always changing
        as an Omnipotent One's goals are rearranging?
Just who are the accomplices, apprentices for a cosmic plan?
How big the bureaucracy, committee? Is God a partisan?

Is God omniscient?   Founder of faith?
Is God all-powerful?   Supernatural wraith?
        Is God monotheistic? An unknowable essence?
        A vengeful God?   Beloved presence?
I'm open to explore many conceptions.
I'm not totally consoled by current selections.

Steer Clear

Steer your way through the ruins of the Altar and the Mall
Steer your way through the fables of Creation and the Fall
Steer your way past the Palaces that rise above the rot...
Leonard Cohen

Steer clear of Altars and Mall
places of exclusion and illusions.
Clear up Creation and the Fall
ideas with confusion, no conclusions.
Palatial and political power rots.
Greater gaps between haves and have nots.

Places of exclusion and illusions
deceive our senses and intelligence,
lure us with tempting intrusions,
play with our sentience and conscience,
tug us toward negative emotions,
plug us with pain-killing potions.

Clear up Creation and the Fall.
Earthbound experience has questions.
We're part of some cosmic protocol
without many helpful suggestions?
Keeping Earthlings bound in fear
will not allow our vision to clear.

Ideas hold confusion, no conclusions
yet we strive to uncover mysteries.
Any upcoming knowledge fusions
to enhance better discoveries?
We cling to what we hope is solid,
even when thoughts are not valid.

Palatial and political power rots.
It's a time of change and extremes.
People detect devious plots.
Everyone wants to fulfill dreams.
Theories and dominance shifts.
Pressures for justice uplifts.

Greater gaps between haves and have nots
provoke violent revolutions.
We turn for rescue to astronauts
to find off-planet solutions.
Meanwhile failing institutions
fall behind on restitutions.

One Way

A line is a dot that went for a walk. Lexa and Dan Walsh at art exhibit

How long do I follow a one way street?
Until I get a chance to change direction?
Do I wait until reaching defeat,
before making a different selection?
        Follow dogma despite negative impact?
        Alter approach by a newly perceived fact?

Until I get a chance to change directions
or reach a blocked off dead end,
how do I cope with reflection
upon concepts others depend?
        Ask: Have I lost my way?
        Respond: Yes–something's not okay.

Do I wait until reaching defeat
or keep options open, remain unaligned?
What new discoveries will I greet?
I can only guess how universe is designed.
        I decided I won't pursue a one - way route.
        My curiosity and imagination are in pursuit.

Before making a different selection
I research, peer outside the box.
Search for a temporary intersection,
avoid organizations with locks.
        I want to keep my thoughts free
        from undue restraints, explore openly.

Follow dogma despite negative impact?
Think of the planet and indoctrinated mind,
the destructive, unsustainable act.
Will we seek the life-giving find?
        The world is wounded, suffering.
        Gaia needs care and buffering.

Alter approach by a newly perceived fact
or renewed ancient wisdom still true?
Will we uncover kind ways to react?
Harmonic, peaceful concepts to imbue?
        Is there only one way to believe?
        Look for the high way to receive.

Belief Waves

*Our personal health and relationships to global war and peace, the reality of our
lives is nothing more than our "belief waves" shaping the quantum stuff that
everything is made of. Everything we experience is all related to what we accept
about the world, our capacities, our traits, and ourselves"* Gregg Braden

A new story is emerging from heart-brain connection.
How we answer *who am I?* impacts our choices.
Move from conflict, competition and separation,
turnover to cooperation, connection, unity bring rejoices.
> We are wired to be extraordinary.
> Our experiences are more than ordinary.

How we answer *who am I?* impacts our choices.
Your consciousness and subconsciousness connect.
We hear scientific and spiritual voices.
We have ancient knowledge we can recollect.
> All this sounds very exciting,
> as well as hopeful and inviting.

Move from conflict, competition and separation,
realize we are in this all together.
Create ways for better communication.
Reduce judgment, loosen tether.
> We can learn lessons from our DNA
> and begin living in a new way.

Turnover to cooperation, connection, unity.
The planet's sustainability could be at stake.
Pollution, wars, waste-- a tragedy.
New outlooks and procedures we can take.
> We are not alone on this planet or cosmos.
> In these extreme times, we need to be on our toes.

We are wired to be extraordinary
we are rapidly discovering more we can do.
Institutions that limit us, say the contrary
could deny evidence or a breakthrough.
> Some groups do not want us to empower
> others and take away their power.

Our experiences are more than ordinary
we will understand we are multidimensional.
We'll increase intuition and gain channel ability.
Let's find ways to be sensational.
> Affirmations from science and spirituality
> rejuvenate my dreams and curiosity.

Heart-Brain Connection

The mind is just like a muscle–the more you exercise it, the stronger it gets and the more it can expand.   Idowu Koyenikan

New science says our mind has two parts–
there are neurons in heart and brain.
We are to hone and tune brains and hearts,
marry the two and become stronger again.
    Our electrical and magnetic fields
    when extended we increase yields.

There are neurons in heart and brain
connect and we achieve deeper thought, intuition
empower immune system, see super learning gain,
upping performance of our constitution.
    Both send signals and hold conversations.
    Together they can improve situations.

We are to hone and tune brains and hearts.
Shift awareness from head to heart, heart stronger.
They are both essential mind counterparts.
Heart can reduce stress longer.
    We can reduce adrenalin and cortisol
    and feel more balanced overall.

Marry the two and become stronger again.
Who knew we had to coordinate the two?
Cooperation could create less pain.
Living from the heart is a great clue.
    Heart-brain coherence
    promotes a harmonic resonance.

Our electrical and magnetic fields
effect intelligence and disposition.
Time we put down our shields–
we're wired for intuition.
    We can access what is true for us
    with less pros and cons list fuss.

When extended we increase yields.
Our inner experiences effect beyond self.
Our heart can change our electro-magnetic fields.
Take ancient instructions off the shelf.
    Language to the field can be learned.
    Ask-receive, you'll not be spurned.

The Shining Spark of Truth

The shining spark of truth cometh forth only after the clash of differing opinions.
Baha'i Writings

Why must opinions clash to produce truth?
Truth seems rarely proven or agreed upon.
Why mess with unpleasantness, sleuth
through speculations and dubious opinion?
> We listen to debunkers state their case.
> We'd never have consensus in any place.

Truth seems rarely proven or agreed upon.
Trends and reinterpretations raise questions.
We glow at the latest phenomenon,
eagerly follow some pundit's suggestions.
> I wonder if their motives are pure
> and do they really know for sure?

Why mess with unpleasantness, sleuth
through mysteries we cannot seem to solve,
chasing a concept to find an untruth?
Do truths always tend to resolve?
> Truths can be inconclusive.
> All eternal truths elusive?

Through speculations and dubious opinions,
diehards stake their stance.
Gather staunch, brainwashed minions--
steadfast through changing circumstance.
> Clash conclusions. Closet in ivory tower
> or stupidly give away their personal power.

We listen to debunkers state their case,
grasp at their truths, hold on by fingertips.
Reason and intuition displace
as pontificators lose their grips.
> Truth becomes a crap shoot.
> Many folks just don't give a hoot.

We'd never have consensus in any place
for there are many ways of knowing.
Old ideas new seekers can erase.
Listeners' ignorance or savvy could be showing.
> Truth needs to remain open to interpretation.
> What truth is worth devastating confrontation?

Knowing

Deep knowing is how we are able to see, hear, or feel the truth or a part of truth about a particular person, place, thing, situation or relationship. Direct knowing is when we experience spiritual truths directly. Sara Wiseman

Dwelling in the cloud of unknowing
allows me to remain free, not commit
to stagnant ideas, thoughts not flowing
I want to remain clouded, I admit.
       If my vision we're completely clear.
       I don't think I would be living here.

Allow me to remain free, not commit
to facts or theories not resonant with me
or to ways or believing or ritual habits
inhibiting exploration and creativity.
       When I am not sure of anything,
       I am open to peruse what life can bring.

To stagnant ideas and thoughts not flowing,
I really don't want you to stick around.
I'm into benign turbulence and insights glowing,
not dense, heavy concepts to confound.
       Deep and direct knowing are elusive.
       Cloud of knowing remains inconclusive.

I want to remain clouded, I admit
for to know deeply and directly is really
beyond my experience of the infinite
I'd settle for knowing love...ideally.
       I might end up a deluded guru
       when balmy, spritely days are through.

I don't think I'd be living here,
even with clouds brushed away.
Subconscious doubts would appear.
Unknowingness would sway
       my deep and direct truths' confidence–
       dismissed as faulty evidence.

The Reluctant Ingrate

I'd like to adopt a more grounded point of view,
to accept earthly conditions more gracefully.
I tend to be quizzical and critical, pursue
answers to this cosmic experiment ungratefully.
      Trying to understand life's meaning,
      there's a lot of dross I'm gleaning.

To accept earthly conditions more gracefully
requires I change my current attitude.
This planet's weight is too great for me.
I seek a brighter, higher altitude.
      Okay, 3D is heavy- get used to it.
      Try to be a lighter conduit?

I tend to be quizzical and critical, pursue
creative dreams despite reality's consensus.
Must I seek every mystery's clue?
Am I my consciousness amanuensis?
      Am I a student taking the Earth School Test?
      By whom or committee am I assessed?

Answers to this cosmic experiment, ungratefully
I request. I want the ability to complete the course.
Did I select to participate free-willfully?
Must I persevere or do I have any recourse?
      Is any thought divergence permitted?
      I want to know before I'm committed.

Trying to understand life's meaning--
am I here to gain and share knowledge?
Here to assist Gaia's house-cleaning?
Which teachers should I acknowledge?
      There seems too much suffering
      without sufficient buffering.

There is a lot of dross I'm gleaning.
Even our space junk orbits debris.
Can I hope our outlook's greening
when we screen vision deliberately?
      But I am here, so now what?
      I just can't keep ears, eyes and mouth shut.

Unpredictable Predictions

Prophets and prophetesses reveal their predictions
An art? A science? Creative science fictions?
Some events appear to manifest in the physical.
Other visions remain hidden or metaphysical.

Curious people want to know what's to come.
What challenges will happen? What we'll become?
But even if we know, there is still fear
and as of yet we can't get out of here.

When reading about future predictions
they reveal possible predilections.
The degree of accuracy varies from what they project.
Their inaccuracies we tend to forget.

The probabilities create speculation
items to ponder and for contemplation.
Negative impacts on people and nature.
Changes in climates, cosmic encounters, culture.

Some suggestions appear out of sci/fi–
maybe contain some solutions we might try.
But the cosmic plan is open to change
and control can be outside our range.

Nostradamus wrote quatrains in rhyme.
Many stunning predictions over time.
Apocalyptic angel Baba Vanga was blind
but saw horrors to boggle your mind.

Mark Twain came in and out with Haley's comet,
knew of brother's death when hadn't happened yet.
Psychic twins claim to share a soul.
Jeanne Dixon saw JFK and MLK Jr. toll.

Sleeping prophet Edgar Cayce
makes other predictors appear lazy.
Trance healings over telephone,
he holds extensive archive of his own.

So many scenarios can hit us.
What claims will omit us?
Free will and full discovery?
We can only hope for humanity's recovery.

Many psychics saw twin towers fall. Climate changes emerge.
Temperature rise. Power shifts submerge.
Our old space stations and satellites crash.
Volcanic eruptions, meteors turn us to ash.

Psychics see aliens build colonies under the sea.
Mars and Venus exploited for resources eventually.
Artificial suns collide, cause drought.
Upheavals in politics and religions leave little doubt.

Disease can come from outer space.
Yellow, white, black create a new race.
Global power shifts, we cause wastelands
as our arrogance, violence, negligence expands.

Wars predicted. Polar ice caps melt.
Some of these effects have been felt.
Cosmic accidents, change planetary orbits,
global warming, hunger cause massive obits.

Sometimes psychics predict medical breakthroughs,
time travel, helpful technological news.
But a comet can hit us, causing our end.
How much hope and belief will we suspend?

We clutter our mind with what can be.
We could clear and recycle creatively.
Even when faced with calamity,
we don't get the chance to react protectively.

We might exploit other planets, colonize Mars.
No idea what our roles are in the stars.
Multiple dimensions, universes could await.
I don't ever expect a clear, clean slate.

No matter the circumstances and our plight–
out of energy and consciousness I seek light.
I can only attempt to do my best
and let the cosmos orchestrate the rest.

Going With the Flow

The past is never still, just like the present is never still. We are always moving in Flow until our next now. Let it all go and let the river of life take you to your next Now. Sara Wiseman

Go with the Flow!
Do we have a choice of direction?
The river of wavering Now–
do we have course selection?
      Past and present never still.
      How much of life is free will?

Do we have a choice of direction
when river forks, tumbles into sea?
When we choose our branch–a perfection
of banking our eventual destiny?
      Rapids, pools and waterfalls
      change challenges and protocols.

The river of wavering Now
tries to see around bend or curve.
Will we steer with enough know-how?
Are we ready to follow-through or swerve?
      Do we guide a paddle or larger boat
      to keep our GPS afloat?

Do we have course selection
or is someone else at controls?
Do we have a goal or predilection
or does our subconscious create our roles?
      Rocks and riverteeth–perhaps hiding
      can be obstacles to our deciding.

Past and present never still.
Energy and consciousness are eternal.
Does our soul express our will?
Does life flourish from each kernel?
      The Flow moves on ready or not.
      Water is essential to people's plot.

How much of life is free will?
Rivers carve canyons, flood.
We can swim or skate icy chill.
Rivers race like our blood.
      The river metaphor may be stale–
      but hope deserts don't prevail.

Conclusions

My only conclusion is I haven't committed
to any conclusion, I remain open.
Some ideas I have completely omitted,
just does not resonate when considered again
       I should not judge others, say what's right.
       I'll try to choose what leans toward light,

To any conclusion, I remain open
for reinterpretation, new insights.
I reject some dark, murky concepts, then
concentrate on positive delights.
       If I have the choice, why not use it?
       If I am given power, don't abuse it.

Some ideas I have completely omitted.
My sentience, though limited, won't buy it.
My biases and rejections I have admitted,
I'm not likely conned with "just try it".
       Conclusions about anything means adhering
       to your resolutions–cheering or fearing?

Just does not resonate when considered again,
my instincts and intuition feel barred.
I witness chaotic events and pain.
I don't want my soul scarred.
       Who I am and what's my role?
       These conclusions would make me whole.

I should not judge others, say what's right
for they have their lives to puzzle out.
They may be better connected, more erudite.
Still, I might want to muzzle them or shout.
       But each is responsible for one's existence,
       (I think) and to interfere might meet resistance.

I'll try to choose what leans toward light,
toward kindness, creativity, cooperation, peace
as I try to best interpret diverse paths-- despite
not concluding the best for me or all. Maybe a piece,
       a glimmer will keep my life upbeat--
       dreaming, yearning, curious, never complete.

Beneath the Clouds

On the Witness Stand

Ideas rose in clouds;
I felt them collide
until pairs interlocked.
so to speak,
making a stable foundation.

Henri Poincare

Seeking Silver Linings

Silver crowns this crone's head's
hair sprouting out thin, silver threads.
At Rio they are bald or in dreds.

At the Olympics they are seeking gold.
(Most drug-free I've been told).
But silver and bronze contenders also bold.

While the athletes perform magnificently,
I deal with much less agility,
use my mind to my best ability.

Silver in my walker and wheelchair
aids me getting from here to there.
I benefit from silver husband's care.

Beyond body to exploring curiosity,
seeking greater luminosity,
my silver crutches reduce pomposity.

Silver in space craft, in my rings,
many expressions silver brings:
coins, silverware and many bejeweled things.

Silver is symbol of 25th anniversary,
We have celebrated 55-- past gold actually.
Silver is used in soldering and photography.

Gold has many more uses, variety,
used for golden opportunity.
I like golden mean preferably.

But I am a silver-Smith.
This is the reality I live with,
creating my own myth.

I seek silver linings, head in cloud
of unknowing, some peeking allowed.
Silver lining route, I've creatively followed.

Surreal: 2016 Word of the Year.

Surrealism: to release creative potential of the unconscious mind. For example by the irrational juxtaposition of images...combining unrelated images in unrelated images or events in a very strange and dreamlike way. Bing

European poets, painters and filmmakers
around 1924 created the surrealist movement.
They sought access to truths of the unconscious mind
by breaking down rational thought--
seems surreal is the perfect word for 2016.

After terrorist attacks, school and street shootings,
suicides and deaths, war traumas,
moments of shock and tragedy,
Merriam-Webster said surreal captured a year
"marked by intense irrational reality of a dream,
or unbelievable, fantastic."

Peter Soklowski, Merriam-Webster editor
thought surreal "a concrete response,
a political response and finally
a philosophical response. That's
what connects all these tragic events."
Other choices: "post- truth" and "xenophobic".

I am a fan of surrealism in art,
but not a fan of living in a surreal reality.
I'm all for boundary-breaking, system-busting,
if the result creates better conditions, visions
for humanity, the planet, the cosmos.

How many surreal situations must we endure?
How much pain, injustice in this Earth School?
Can consensual reality become surreally harmonic?
Can people up their vibes, tweak their DNA,
create a world not cramped by limitations?

Promises of divine and alien interventions
are a long time in coming, clutched in hierarchies,
rigmarole, delayed manifestations and activations.
Any level of consciousness or sentience for clarity
in this surreal cosmic experiment? Bring on the light!

Deeds not Words

The suffragette slogan has many deeds--
still not complete around the world.
We have not met women's needs.
Too many women remain unfurled.
> The statistics reveal inequality.
> Men in power, the majority.

Still not complete around the world
is power over their bodies or vote.
Paid less, as poverty swirled,
culture clutches at their throat.
> Why must women have to fight
> for what should be a human right?

We have not met women's needs,
in health care, access to education.
Caught in war as family bleeds,
they face an unjust, dire situation.
> Women give men life, their birth,
> then men blast and mine the Earth.

Too many women remain unfurled
their voices silenced, their words
unheeded, intentions hurled.
Men, more concerned with boards.
> Not all men treat women unfairly--
> but equal opportunity is achieved, rarely.

The statistics reveal inequality,
but numbers alone don't curtail her fate.
It is hierarchies, cultural, sexist plurality,
out-dated ideas we need to update.
> It's what's in our hearts and heads--
> it's empowerment a privileged man dreads.

Men in power, the majority
might talk the talk, but not assist deeds--
they don't want to risk perceived superiority.
Time to revise global creeds.
> Power to womyn over their own lives.
> Do so and the planet thrives.

Current Currency

Since we are updating and revising currency
away from the pale males to a woman of color,
let's make all our bills more vibrant hues,
pieces of art, cosmic graphic, not just patriotic commerce.

Slave abolitionist Harriet Tubman replaced
slave-holder president Andrew Jackson--.
She is someone of substance not
one of our problematic presidents.

Many folks poked and shunned
$20 bills, for Jackson also pushed
Indian Removal Act through Congress.
How about some role models on bills?

Other nations have beautiful bills.
Why does USA display masonic symbols
and show little of our rich diversity.
Credit cards do not look any better.

If we have to deal with current currency
no wonder so many people shop on-line,
pay their bills automatically, avoid cash.
Nothing lures people to look at money.

They did try some state-designed quarters,
token Sacajawea dollars, which some people collected.
But mostly bills and coins get tucked away in banks
and pockets, not meant for display.

I would like an artistic miniature,
a memorable quote or poem on bills.
Something to enjoy reflecting on
before spending. Light-energy released.

I'd have bills in bulky pockets and purse
to draw out to explore amid cell phones,
tablets, computers, Pokemon Go--
the screen scene while waiting.

Tranquilly, I'd ponder each splendiferous bill,
truly missing them each expenditure, its departure.
Now I pay bills with just a momentary glance
to see that the amount is correct and whine.

Benny-Factor

Secret benefactor leaving $100 bills in Salem Oregon.

Many people find $100 they insist
came from mysterious philanthropist.
Over $50,000 in $100 bills
found in stores and at festivals.

Into breakfast cereals, diapers-- folded bill tucked
even into a feminine hygiene product.
The "benny-ed" have been helped in beneficial ways:
pay bills, meds, toys or find giving back pays.

Beneficent Ben Franklin with a smiling face
is bringing happiness all over the place.
Fred Meyer has 156 Benny bills found.
A Saturday Market vendor re-passed ten around.

Needy beneficiaries seem to find the money
from the Benny Santa-Easter Bunny.
Some donate their cash to charity, non-profits.
For three years Salem has serendipitous benefits.

Women and children seem to be Benny's target,
but all ages and backgrounds discover bills in market.
Often acts of kindness are noticed and applauded.
Benny remains anonymous, but still lauded.

Each of us can imagine who Benny might be–
a Benita? Benjamin? Beyonce-type celebrity?
The intention gives me hope for broader beneficence–
more benefaction of benevolent significance.

Challenges

A woman I know has two
mentally challenged, grown children
and is divorced from an abusive husband.

The daughter is developmentally delayed
and receives support from my son's
agency which serves people through
what he calls the county's
Developmental Diversity Program.

Her son is in a psych ward
suffering a psychic break.
He is locked up. She dances with him
to calm him down when she visits.

Despite all these challenges
she is upbeat and sometimes
sees humor in her situation.

She is writing two books about
her children and the struggles
to get them the care they need.
She hopes her books will help
others dealing with similar conditions.

Another woman I know
has a mentally unstable daughter.
who likes to live outdoors
and takes medicine unreliably.
This mother is also writing a book
of her journey with her daughter.
She also wants to help other families
who face similar hurdles.

I have given both women
each other's email so they can meet,
share their stories and discoveries.
I wonder why there must be such stress
and unhappiness in this world?

Writers are supposed to have tension
in their work to propel word to word
line by line, sentence by sentence,
paragraph or stanza down the page--
earthly experiences to connect with
and learn by–endure whatever the odds.

Why is suffering needed
in this cosmic experiment in duality?
Why can't we be equipped
with all the skills to manifest our dreams?
Why must we learn compassion
by problems and misfortune?
Why the flaws? Why not just joy
and love in a peaceful, creative, world?

When can we move away from negativity?
When can we evolve to engage positively?
Why must these two women
and all the people and essences
in this world face conflict, fear and sadness?

How many experiments are there in the cosmos?
Are Earthlings being tested for some reason?
Are we making progress?
When I think of all the afflicted people,
are they the guinea pigs? Are we all?
Perhaps mad scientists are in control?
Have they enough data to make a diagnosis?
Do they care about the chaos, violence,
wasted potential of the subjects they control?

If we really had free will, how many people
would choose to develop with such pain?
On a fairer playing field, with better equipment,
supportive rules, we could play the game of life,
reach our goals– not competing-all winning.

Long Lines

We drove through thick fog
toward Portland for Scan Fair.
Sun poked through briefly in Salem.

Portland's concrete overpasses,
and low Jersey barriers were fringed
with dark smudges as if moldy.

Tall walls spider-webbed
with dormant vines- scraggly
black etchings on gray loomed.

We parked in a large garage
and joined a long line to be
searched before entry to the fair.

The Veteran's Coliseum
is cavernous. The rest rooms,
when found, sprout rusty toilets.

Tickets for the craft fair
could be purchased one floor down
at the end of another line.

Once inside the delightful, creative
crafters, wafts of meatballs, cookies,
performers singing and dancing–joyous.

We did not know under leaden sky
Portland Women 's March Against Hate
meandered through downtown with colorful signs.

There have been many parades
against Trump in Portland. This march
started at Director Park in chilled air.

The next day I read the Fallen Angels
Choir sang, politicians and activists spoke,
expressing hope for protecting diversity.

Portland is a sanctuary city.
Mothers wanted their children to know
Portland supports and loves everybody.

We drove home through urban grime.
Spits of rain heading south
until we reached our suburban home.

I placed my Scandinavian purchases
mostly angels, tomte and a laser-cut Lucia
into my light-bringing collections.

In my warren of hope, I renewed my vow,
to join the Portland's Women's March in January
and wear a safety pin until then.

The Imprint of Andy Warhol Prints
The idea of waiting for something makes it more exciting. Andy Warhol

Wandering through the Andy Warhol exhibit
of 250 pieces sprawled on three floors
of the Portland Art Museum, did not
ignite excitement, more puzzlement.

We did a lot of waiting for a slow elevator
after first floor multi-colored combos of Mao.
Volunteers earnestly screened prints while,
above slides flashed of Mao's transformations.

On the third floor was Marilyn Monroe amid
Jimmy Carter, Liza Minnelli, JFK, and Jackie,
Mick Jagger splayed with splattered variations.
Of course the Campbell soup cans and dress.

Somehow plucking photos from magazines,
newspapers, from ads and television to Pop art,
multi-screening over-hues- so mechanical and commercial
does not excite warmth or engagement from me.

The second floor had some porno picks
of uplifted penis over anus and other black and white
shots of limited appeal. His more whimsical drawings
of shoes, cats–nature topics were more playful.

Warhol said, "Isn't life a series of images
that change as they repeat themselves?"
Sara Krajewski said he tried "to the enthrall eye,
incite action and elicit desire." Pop-eyed? Cock-eyed?

Repetition through printmaking and reproduction
whether with political posters, celebrity obsession,
may be pop art, but when he's not copying media,
manipulating photos, and draws his own– art pops.

Mermaid Parade

First Portlandia Mermaid Parade. Poet's Beach, Portland, Oregon
"helping people reconnect with that childhood level of joy." Una the Mermaid

200 mermaids and mermen
flipper and fin

flipped and flopped in summer sun--
fun and fancy run.

Sequins, seashells, spray-colored hair,
smiles everywhere.

Flaunting merfolk's nautical flare,
pirates, jellyfish tag-a-longs,
lured by playful sea sirens' songs.
Flipper and fin, fun and fancy run, smiles everywhere.

Cosplay at Comic-Con

Bing splayed a Cosplay at Comic-Con--
costumes from the realm of imagination,
a fantastic phenomenon,
Earthlings in cosmic creation.
>Big Bang Theory is my geek cred.
>These characters are so talented.

Costumes from the realm of imagination
manifested from comic books and screen.
Super powers, cosmic configurations
all gussied up to make the scene.
>Skin tinted many colors accepted.
>Genders empowered, hope projected.

A fantastic phenomenon
to see people pondering alternative futures,
cosmic beings to wonder upon,
considering other universal cultures.
>The good guys and gals win
>in these stories we imagine.

Earthlings in cosmic creation
experience a shift in viewpoint, new vision.
Comic-Con is more than recreation.
It is a place to dream, an essential provision.
>You can be you, any way you
>chose to express by what you do.

Big Bang Theory is my geek cred-
comic book store, Justice League, Star Trek,
I'm lured by laughter, my awe fed
by the writing, the acting, the intellect.
>Show stirs my earthly and cosmic admiration,
>though Comic Con is not my destination.

These characters are so talented
I share their worlds and feel free
to relax, smile, feel contented
to explore my own creativity.
>So Comic-Con characters on cosplay,
>your parade brightened this sunny day.

Loie and Her Muses

Loie Fuller was an innovative dancer
        experimenter with lighting,
new ways to dance–a ballet of light.

"Fairy of Light", she swished wands
        extending her arms like wings, flowing white silk
splashed with multi-colors on the stage.

Loie ran, turned, jumped across the stage
        moving light and fabric alone
or with seven dancers, her Muses.

Old film from the turn of the century
        hints at the sensation she caused
with her enhanced serpentine skirt dances.

Luminous images in gauzy gowns, wispy--
        yet with strenuous movements from her core
imbued energy to the fabric and dance.

"Orgy of Luminosity", "Goddess of Light"--
        modern dancers today still are your Muses,
like flames of colored light, space stars, rolling clouds.

Natural Disaster Postage Stamp Sculpture

Art should be weirder than watercolor. Bill Varsell

When cousin Bill weathers a storm,
blizzard, hurricane, nor'easter,
he retrieves a suitcase
scavenged from a dumpster
while clearing the home of a nutty, hoarded aunt.
The suitcase was filled with 1940-50's engraved stamps.
He considered them quirky and colorful.
He thought he might do something with them someday.

To stave boredom during a storm
without power for days, Bill created
3-D funky, fantasy, mini-sculpture
from layering canceled postage stamps.
With a razor knife, he cut out elements
he used for his mini-art collection
which hangs on the dining room wall.
Two cent stamps cover the frame.
Postal stamp art became a natural disaster tradition.

Kind of like taxidermy, he uses cardboard
from the bottom of a notepad and a small stick
of wood with sandpaper glued on to carve a face,
then compresses eye sockets with a tweezer handle.
The stamps' skin is stretched over it,
giving the face a 3-D effect,
takes a second or two to stand out.
Your mind loosens, inanimate objects
appear to come to life. He intends
to experiment with "Stamp Taxidermy"
in a forthcoming natural disaster.

In a recent storm he added adornments
from stamps to a 19th century photo,
so the mother and child garments
were as colorful as the floral frame.
Using his magnifying head piece,
Bill pops color, recombines a sculptural collage
as wind wails, rain or snow slathers his home.

The New Swimsuit

At a trade show I am selling
a new innovation in swimsuits–
light, aero-dynamic, breathable,
covering the limbs like a scuba diver–
more like a second skin.

Other venders carp at me
challenging its excellence,
saying it should be banned
from competition because
of an unfair advantage.

Irritated, I decide to take a break,
seek my husband to staff the booth
for awhile. I find him about to board a bus.
He is eager to do his own projects
and does not want to substitute.

Heading back to the booth,
I come upon a small auditorium
with a play in progress.
I am not only expected to join the audience
but to play a part in the play.

They are in a Nazi compound.
I ask if my part is an evil Nazi--
a bombastic bully like Trump.
I ask my character's name
and a copy of the script.

When no lines arrive, I stealthily
creep out of the room, dodging usher-guards
by hiding behind curtains, until
I reach an open room where a woman
holds a baby outside a window.

The baby smiles, relieved
I have returned to my station.
But the room appears empty,
no swim suits, husband, so
must not have found the stall yet.

Conversations of the day invade
this night dream: Picnic gab-fests,
many Rio Olympic swim meets.
Michael Phelps and our American teams
manage to be golden without my new swimsuits.

They Are Tenting Again

The Smiths are setting up paper tents
to lure my moth and buggy kin.
These tents have lethal contents.
We must not go within.
>Why can't we co-exist?
>Why must the Smiths resist?

To lure my moth and buggy kin
to go inside a toxic enclave
they put attractants to our chagrin.
Not a friendly way to behave.
>We don't bug them very much,
>maybe a nuisance flutter, tiny touch.

These tents have lethal contents.
Smiths hide them everywhere.
They hold murky portents.
The Smiths are aware and don't care
>tents are deadly, keep their vow
>to stick us to the walls somehow.

We must not go within.
We must not fly like a fool.
We must learn and begin
to evade their cruel tool.
>If they don't want us around
>we should find a new compound.

Why can't we co-exist?
We tease the breeze, plop a dot.
But we must go they insist
to another nesting, resting spot.
>Can't they see our time is short?
>Can't they be a better sport?

Why must the Smiths resist
our brief encounters in shared hearth?
But their temporary tents persist.
They won't give us a safe berth.
>We view their efforts as unkind
>and hope they have a change of mind.

Catty Catastrophes

Some cronies in my exercise class live alone.
They want feline company at home.
They want a companion and beloved of their own.
A cat to race to the door in welcome.
>They regale the pets' adventures and expense.
>They put up with inconceivable nonsense.

They want feline company at home--
a cat to share their beds and laps,
a warm, furry fuzz ball to comb,
someone to care for. Perhaps
>they overlook the costs, unaware
>of the inconveniences they share.

They want a companion and beloved of their own--
someone to stroke, fuss over. They overlook
ripped furniture and curtains, litter box odors. I'm mind blown
over repairs, vet bills, house hazards they undertook.
>Cat fights, cat mischief, cat sneezes, cat stumbles--
>a long list of mishaps and messy feline fumbles.

A cat to race to the door in welcome
is worth placing plastic all over,
cat-proofing until obstacles overcome.
They are prone to becoming a push-over.
>Cats drink from toilets
>even slurp from faucets.

They regale the pets' adventures and expense
replace broken objects, cat-tossed false teeth,
hearing aids gone rogue, new scratching offense,
wear cat shirts. Are they seething underneath?
>I've no patience for a cat.
>I won't become their door mat.

They put up with inconceivable nonsense,
just to have some cats frisking about.
I'm sure their intentions to them make sense.
It's their sanity that is in doubt.
>Maybe they have not realized yet
>it is they who became the pet.

Under a Cloudless, Blue Sky

yard art shines in sun
across sidewalk chunks
bordering the lawn

snails, turtle, hedgehog
wild animal replicas
heron, peacock pose

yellow-winged pink pig
butterfly whirligig whirls
among the wildlings

transitory birds
briefly on leafy branches
robins, jays, black birds

LBJ's perch, stare
at stilled, muted, strange neighbors

Cloud-Window-Watcher

Clouds
pass by
my
window
as I rest,
changing
shape,
texture,
density,
pushing sky-scapes
frame by frame–
movie
screen
for me.
Images
stories
to
create
joy.

Full Moon Christmas 2016

Wide-eyed, white full moon
eye-lided by clouds
moonshine on Christmas lights
winking in the dark.

Not until 2034
will there be another
full moon on Christmas
staring silently.

The moon follows us
as we drive quieted streets
lined with multicolored, lighted homes.
We have candles in our windows.

Cloud-Gathering

2016 Elections

*To penetrate and dissipate
these clouds of darkness,
the general mind must be
strengthened by education.*

Thomas Jefferson

On a Wing and a Prayer

Our thoughts and prayers are not enough. Barack Obama

President Obama sweats the reminder of his term.
The next president soon to be decided.
Voters uneasy about possible successor squirm.
Citizens wonder how the candidates became so lopsided.
      Thoughts and prayers are not enough.
      Neither campaigner appears up to snuff.

The next president soon to be decided
causes hostile reactions from supporters.
Ideologies, personalities, agendas collided.
Advocates for choice or anti-aborters--
      whatever the circumstance,
      antagonisms, differences advance.

Voters uneasy about possible successor squirm.
Obama's firmly in Hillary's camp.
Barack is a lame duck wanting to affirm
his legacy with a Democratic stamp.
      He champions women, minorities, health,
      strong economy, world peace, more equity in wealth.

They wonder how the candidates became so lopsided--
Janus-headed in opposite directions.
Their characters called into question. Blindsided
public is angry, divided, dislikes selections.
      Trump is a despot, racist, sexist groper.
      Clinton loses trust, victim of email interloper.

Thoughts and prayers are not enough.
Anxiety grips as citizenry seethes.
We want a president made of finer stuff.
Lies, deception and distrust leaves
      country split on election's impact.
      Will the actual winner, win in fact?

Neither campaigner appears up to snuff
to unite the nation and confront our issues.
Obama knows the next president has it rough.
When he departs, many of us with damp tissues.
      Self-promoter Trump would create global distress.
      We need a hard-working woman to clean up the mess.

Hope or Hate

> 2016 Republican and Democratic Conventions

Cleveland, then Philadelphia
> sheer mania

Dump Trump. Pillory Hillary
> arbitrary

Voters choose to spew hope or hate--
> participate

Separate or cooperate.
Qualified with experience--
one displays her intelligence.
Sheer mania, arbitrary. Participate!

The Will of the People

As democracy is perfected, the office of president represents more and more closely,
the inner soul of the people. On some great and glorious day the plain folks of the
land will reach their heart's desire at last and the White House will be adorned by a
downright moron. H.L. Mencken

Could we have dimmed so quickly?
The will of the people really served
so undemocratically?
Did Americans get whom they deserved?
     Trump doesn't represent our nation's soul.
     Voters' apathy and turnout played a role.

The will of the people really served
when only 25% voted for Trump?
Hillary received the popular vote. We observed
the moronic behavior of that bullying chump.
     But voter turnout was only 56%
     for candidates many people resent.

So undemocraticallly
elected by Electoral College--
so systematically
each vote they don't acknowledge.
     Some votes count more in some states,
     followed by contentious, deplorable debates.

Did Americans get who they deserved?
Don't they want health care, hard fought rights?
Trash treaties, pollute environment, disturbed
by diversity, self-empowerment? Choose blights?
     If some people think nation is unjust and unfair
     why turn to a tax-evading, bankrupting billionaire?

Trump doesn't represent our nation's soul
numerically or from our hearts.
We can't step back to dark-side control.
Each must step up, forward and play the parts.
     Act beyond hope to effect change.
     Keep justice within our range.

Voters' apathy and turnout played a role.
We can't just watch injustice take over.
This mess pollsters couldn't accurately poll.
Democracy needs a massive make over.
     We must watch closely- impeach--
     if his groping tiny hands overreach.

The Electoral College Must Go

Our truest response to the irrationality of the world is to paint, sing or write, for only in such response do we find truth.   Madeliene L'Engle

We can't just paint, sing, write the election away.
We must protest the injustice, advocate for change.
The Electoral College is unfair in every way.
Two recent Presidents won popular vote. Exchange
      and Gore and Clinton could have kept peace.
      Must we wait for irrationality to increase?

We must protest the injustice, advocate for change
creativity and arts are part of reconstruction.
We must look at problems with a wider range,
find ways to reduce the fear and destruction.
      I hope the protests and requests go national--
      all points of view seek fairness and the rational.

The Electoral College is unfair in every way.
A few states' voters have more impact.
Electors and pollsters have too much say.
Popular voters choice denied in fact.
      Urban and rural voters each get one vote.
      White men control, I should note.

Two recent Presidents won popular vote. Exchange
system to one vote per voter. Ease access
and see turnout and results rearrange.
Only when fair is democracy a success.
      Ignoring climate change and hard won gains,
      depends on which political party hold reins.

And Gore and Clinton could have kept the peace
Gore protects climate, Hillary women's rights.
Obama's progress destroyed piece by piece
by Conservative Whites ignoring other's plights.
      Can we unite to face the challenge
      or wait for left-out people's revenge?

Must we wait for irrationality to increase?
To paint, sing, write is not enough.
Pent up global concern is ready to release
if we abandon treaties, don't bring right stuff.
      The Electoral College does not reflect us.
      Popular vote advocates–make a fuss!

Every Vote Should Count

Al Gore and Hillary Clinton had the popular vote.
The electoral college gives more weight
to some states and voters, doesn't devote
any regard to Guam, other places. They can debate
       but their vote does not count.
       Our anger should mount.

The electoral college gives more weight
to rural, less populated places.
Times have changed. Despite your state
each vote should count equally, displaces
       original **forefathers** (some slavery owners)
       concept of democracy. Are we postponers?

To some states and voters, devote
attention to each vote cast.
We have a new world vision to promote.
Without equal, informed voters, it won't last.
       If we had elected Al Gore,
       we could have avoided the Iraq War.

Any regard to Guam, other places–they can debate
but citizens have no impact. No electoral vote there.
We need balance. We should reinstate
       one vote per citizen for everyone, everywhere.
       If we had elected Hillary Clinton
       enlightened action not forbidden.

But their vote does not count
if we keep Electoral College.
Our government should have to account
for inequities and all could acknowledge
       brainwashed people could free themselves
       from undemocratic ideas. Put them on archaic shelves.

Our anger should mount
as we see our votes, system disregards.
Special interests, out-dated concepts discount
disenfranchised citizens the Old School retards
       I am devastated at our nation's backward thrust.
       In America–I give hope, but no longer trust.

Calling Trump Names

The surname Trump refers to trumpeters
or makers of trumpets.
I'm not in the Trump band.

Perhaps Trumpets refer to horny, greedy
males who manipulate others
and can't keep their hands to themselves.

Perhaps Trumpettes are un-empowered
females who consider their fates out of their hands
and are manipulated by tradition.

Perhaps Trum-pets are cronies favored by Trump
and his other animal pets or Putin
and other overseas pals currying favor.
Trump renames buildings globally with his name.

The Electoral College did not dump Trump
even though the popular vote did.
The Electoral College crumped on their duty
to protect the nation from misguided voters.
Remember Hitler was elected legally.

Is this just a bump in the road of democracy?
How did we let our vigilance slump?
Unfit cabinet chumps and loyal lumps of clay,
won't get us over the hump of despair.

Trump spews racist, sexist, xenophobic trash
from the stump, thrumps minorities,
clumps misinformation into Tweets.

Trump treats women like strumpets.
Be glad you are a frump. Trump's less likely
to grab you inappropriately.
He criticizes those who are plump.

Pundits suggest we not jump to conclusions.
Even though he is a pain in the rump to Progressives
and he re-clumps rewards for the top 1%.

This offensive grump
is a champion mugwump.
Many want to thrump Trump thinking.

Forrest Gumps and illnesses like mumps
protections may be trumped by Trump policies.
Are we going to allow the USA to become a Trumpland?
Here comes trumpeter swan song Donald – duck?

Verklempt
   to be overwhelmed by emotion. Oxford English Dictionary

The OED is the guide to history, meaning
and pronunciation to over 829,000 words, senses
and compounds from English-speaking world.
They have quarterly updates like verklempt
which with another new word Brexit
seems to express temper of the times.

At victory rallies Trump tries to tamp tone
of his "vicious, violent, screaming" supporters.
Now his opponents protest mostly non-violently
but loudly, after the shock has worn off.
All the upheaval, hacking, commotion
leaves people puzzled, panicked, drained.

The President-elect uses twitter un-presidentially.
He called China's capture of our drone "unpresidented"
when he should have said "unprecedented".
Many citizens wish he could be "unpresidented".
His campaign and aftermath "unprecedented".
The whole political scene makes populace verklempt.

I must add verklempt to my rhyming dictionary
with dreamt, tempt, attempt, kempt, contempt,
pre-empt, exempt, unkempt, undreamt.
I never dreamt, such a man would attempt,
to exempt his taxes, speak of women with contempt,
tempt rise of alt-right, pre-empt popular vote. Undreamt.

New Trumpland

Like a bird on a wire, like a drunk in a midnight choir I have tried in my way to be free. Leonard Cohen

I have not walked a tightrope, never learned to fly.
I have never been drunk, left church and know why.
>I have tried in my way to be free.

I champion women's choice and demand equal rights.
I champion the environment, care about all people's plights.
>I have tried in my way to be free.

All the ists and isms keep thoughts diverse,
but for communicating often make things worse.
>I have tried in my way to be free.

A friend said she leaves it all in God's hands.
Do we have free will or follow a God's commands?
>I have tried in my way to be free.

In Trump's tiny hands scratching narcissistic head
he gropes, divides, denies rights, insults instead.
>I have tried in my way to be free.

In a Democracy we are supposed to separate
and be free of domination by religion or state.
>I have tried in my way to be free.

We have a whole planet to nurture
if our descendants have a future.
>I have tried in my way to be free.

Trump's policies must be rejected.
Remember Hitler was legally elected.
>I have tried in my way to remain free.

Might doesn't t make right. Hate is not great.
Best intentions must support electorate.
>I have tried in my way to remain free.

The Electoral College gave us New Trumpland,
though popular vote Hillary won. I understand
>I will have to revise Democracy to remain free.

The Enlightened States of America

Due to the election, e-mails suggest
certain Blue States should secede.
California and Oregon could become Jefferson
or include all the Blue States and proceed.

Blue states prefer to be progressive,
care for the environment, civil rights.
Leave conservative, Old Order behind!
We like to drive forward on brights.

In the Enlightened States of America
the popular vote candidate wins.
Get rid of greedy, outmoded institutions!
The age of the equal citizen begins.

The statistics for the Blue States are better.
85% of venture capital and entrepreneurs,
best colleges, produce food, fruit and wine,
80% of fresh water, redwoods, sequoias and condors.

Lower divorce rate than Christian Coalition's
less control over women's bodies or all minds.
Reds can have tornadoes, hurricanes, pollution,
alt-right media, place where tradition binds.

The Rust Belt run by robots, find jobs gone.
Fracked and piped sending Asia your resources,
Red States find options, infrastructure decayed,
prey to political, economic, religious forces.

Red States looked to a tax-dodging billionaire
to drain the swamp and straighten things out.
His cabinet is generals, not-qualified loyalists
with failed resumes and climate change doubts.

If the Blue States create their own union-- bolt
from the Divided States of America, Red States beware,
you'll wake up disillusioned, you better re-empower--
democracy, health care, protections won't be there.

Rebels from the Red States you might have to move,
go to the states with a different hue.
Or we could get our nation's act together
and unite to a cooperative, positive view.

Safety Pins

People who stand against
racism, sexism, xenophobia,

for the rights of those with disabilities,
minorities, LGBTQ, refugees,

in the wake of the election,
Americans join folks who oppose Brexit's

discrimination to wear safety pins,
to say you are safe with me.

Safety pins are a symbol
no one should be treated unfairly

because of race, gender, beliefs.
Those of # notmypresident views

advocate civil disobedience,
nonviolent mass protests, strikes,

urge perseverance and audacity.
Let others know what you stand for.

Displaying a safety pin
to commit to help, defend

and stand up for justice
is another statement.

Wear safety pins
on your hat, your purse

your shirt, sweater, coat
on the loop of your jeans.

Whatever your wearing--
put a pin on it.

Maybe add net for a safety net.
Maybe neon to glow in the dark.

Maybe enlarge and embellish
to invent new sizes, shapes, connections--

Wear it as a fashion statement.
Kindness is always in fashion.

Perhaps they will be on bumper stickers,
adorn signs in shops, beside the road.

Twitter #safetypin movement
for more options

if Trump impinges
on civil and human rights.

Safety pins hold cloth diapers,
pieces of a quilt pattern, crafts,

a missing button-- anything
needing connection, support.

Multicolored safety pins,
some with bright-colored plastic clasps.

Safety pins and bead jewelry, ornaments,
bracelets, necklaces, decorative pins--even angels.

Safety pins can be used by everyone--
too many connotations for zippers.

Like the white-face clowns
who responded to White Supremacist shouts

of "white power?" by tossing "white flowers",
"white flour" then held signs of "wife power",

safety pins are another way
to be in solidarity with groups

who feel unsafe after the Trumpocalypse--
another way to stick it to them.

Bring on the Clowns

ARA (Anti Racist Action) clowns block confronts VNN (Vanguard Nazi/KKK) in Knoxville, Tennessee 2016

VNN Hate Rally met ARA clowns.
White-face clowns, some in tutus
danced and pranced toward march.

White Supremacists shouted "white power!"
at the clowns. Behind their masks
its hard to tell the color of clown's skin.

"White Power!" shouts met
with clowns retort "White flower?"
and tossed white flowers at them.

"White Power!" shouts met
with clowns' question- "white flour?"
then spilled flour over the marchers.

"White Power" shouts met
with dancing clowns– "tight shower?"
and lifted solar shower in the air.

"White Power!" shouts met
"Wife power!" as the female clowns
lifted male clowns in response.

VNN members were enraged,
clutching hearts like heart attack,
bulging eyes and veins in their rage.

Alex Lindner, VNN founder
was arrested and carried by four cops
passed the red, shiny shoes of the clowns.

Masked or not, face evil. Nonviolently
protest for the majority of decent people
who wear safety pins over their hearts.

Uncle Sam Bow to the Aunties

Two women important to our culture were pretty much ignored in the election. One is Lady Liberty and the other is Mother Earth....These two women could use more attention from everyone in our culture.   Court Smith

The Statue of Liberty apparently will not welcome
as many tired, poor masses yearning to be free.
Newcomers by land could face a wall.

Civil rights, justice and progress won after years of struggle
can be erased by a conservative Congress,
25% of the voters and mostly white men.

Mother Earth, gouged and gasping for air
faces increased mining, more pollution
of air, land and seas, fracking-induced earthquakes.

We could withdraw from global environmental treaties,
by the greed of the climate change deniers,
become warlike Ugly Americans again.

Why didn't the women stand up to protect themselves
from groping, sexism, disrespect, no control
over their own body? I'll not rejoin underpowered women.

We still have an archaic top hat as nation's symbol
along with an Electoral College which does not reflect
the popular vote. We need to make positive change.

Take that top hat and tip it to all the people.
Uplift everyone and give Gaia a break.
Trump Tower can crumble, but not the Aunties.

"Nasty Women Get Things Done"

The Women's March planned
at the Lincoln Memorial
for January 21st the day after
the inauguration has been banned
by a massive "omnibus blocking permit"
for days and weeks at many
of the political places in D.C.

Millions of marchers have marched
the mall for justice and their rights.
Women around the country planned
to march in solidarity with D.C.
Women want to protest and protect
justice and civil rights.
This is outright censorship.

In Portland, Oregon women organized
referring to themselves after Hillary–
"Nasty Women Get Stuff Done."
The popular vote did not win
and these women mean business.
The 'S' word can also be "shit"
among those not offended.

They created a poster like a flag
for their Women Against Hate March
in December to channel shock and dismay.
The blue area says: In Our America.
There are eight-stripes
alternating red and white saying:
> All people are equal.
> Love wins.
> Black lives matter.
> Immigrants and refugees are welcome.
> Disabilities are respected.
> Women are in charge of their bodies.
> People and planet are valued over profits.
> Diversity is celebrated.

Social media spread the word.
Posters sold for $10, the profits go toward
making more signs and a housing fund.
Demand is mushrooming and membership
is growing rapidly. I need to join and get a sign,
for when I march in Portland on January 21st.

Bursting the Bubble

In our progressive college town,
we know we live in a bubble.
We work together to make it livable.
We are aware of impending trouble.

Tonight's city council agenda concerns
an environmental plan and sanctuary.
Standing room only, many testify.
Some on the council are a little wary.

Sanctuary city will be decided first.
Citizens tell of need for protections.
Teacher tells of bullied students,
Muslim man fears certain detections.

A black woman endures offensive slurs.
Neo-Nazi man in gym scares Muslim women away.
High school young woman describes her scene.
Spanish translators. Testimonies tend to sway.

Citizens don paper Earth's on ribbon,
wear safety pins on their chest,
quietly listen, state their position.
This is democracy at its best.

After amendments and recommendations
finally the city council takes a vote.
They pass sanctuary and later environment plan.
A victory for many Corvallis folk.

In many towns people are in election shock.
Our town is overwhelmingly Democratic.
We are on alert, don't want our bubble to burst
in a fragile nation, want to remain asymptomatic.

Some towns don't have a bubble to burst--
their environment already blown apart.
Time to repair air, water, earth, souls together
with united actions from the heart.

White Elephant Sale

White elephant is a possession which its owner cannot dispose of and whose cost, particularly that of maintenance, is out of proportion to its usefulness.   Wikipedia

I bought a small, stuffed white elephant for $12.99
with a red top hat, black and white checked saddle
trimmed in red, donning a friendly smile.

An elf dressed in green, rides the elephant.
His pointed hat holds a swig of holly.
Together they stride the hope chest—cheerfully.

Though it is close to election time,
I was not promoting the Republican symbol,
unless it represents a white party ghost.

The Kings of Siam presented out of favor courtiers
who were obnoxious with a white elephant
whose maintenance caused the owner's ruin.

Today a white elephant is an object, scheme,
business venture considered without use or value.
I think of morally and financially bankrupt Trump.

My elephant may collect dust, but exudes happiness.
In Hindu and Buddhist cosmology, white elephants
are important. This elephant celebrates Christmas.

P.T. Barnum billed white elephant Toung Taloung
as "Sacred White Elephant of Burma" but King of Siam
gave him a dirty, gray elephant with a few pink spots.

The British East Africa Company in Uganda
regarded their turbulent presence a white elephant.
Conflict lead to ineffectual administration there.

Again I think of Trump, his smarmy, sleazy deals,
lack of plans to lead a nation-- a true white elephant
the Republicans and regressives let run rogue.

Also, White Elephant Sales are holiday
exchanges at parties and fund-raisers of dumped,
unwanted, not useful, bric-a-brac hopefully for profit.

When it is just a party, these donated, tossed items
might be treasured by someone else...or not.
Sometimes you get stuck and bring it to the next event.

My white elephant is not white elephant trash.
I will treasure this trunked, chunk of pleasure,
maintain him in my heart, even when stored.

My benign white elephant is a seasonal delight,
an angelic white elephant, useful to express joy and light
for a hard world, every season and soft, bright belief.

Seasonal Changes

Time to take down
Thanksgiving decorations
(stoking gratitude)
and exchange, Indians, Pilgrims
and pumpkins for Christmas
(inciting sharing and caring)
with Santas, elves, reindeer
but I have to take out empty
Thanksgiving storage boxes
for full Christmas containers
which is not easy due to both
my bone on bone arthritic knees
(the bane and pain of my existence)
to make all the decorative transfers
of mostly Annalee felt figures,
since the Moon Room which has
many bestrewn fake trees
with hundreds of wooden ornaments,
and international creches, Swedish
figures, Lucias and Star Boys
have been up for three years
to avoid a three-day, back-breaking
transfer situation--so this exchange
is modest in comparison–
just 28 elves upon camel, cow,
llamas, zebras, reindeer, moose,
and goat in Christmasy garb
prancing on the buffet, in addition
to two bathrooms with two tiny trees
dangling small ornaments as well as
counters and toilet tops with creatures
in glittery regalia, while
in living room there's two long
coffee tables with about a hundred
symbols of Christmas and Hanukkah
garbed mostly in red, green and white
to extol the spirit of joy, peace, love
and giving this season evokes, yet
after placing additional creatures
in the tv room like snowman,
polar bear, rhino, gussied up folks,
and the table in "heaven"
housing thousands of angels
in my mini-museum—somehow
my enthusiasm has been doused
by the 2016 Presidential Election,
when popular vote does not count,
reactionary, backward beliefs
will take a toll against Obama's
progressive, progress agenda,
which means this seasonal holiday
before a disastrous inauguration
(I plan to join the Woman's March
either in Portland or DC the next day)
could be the last holiday with hope
lingering and the lights still shining
brightly because the New Year brings
more fear and a call to resist,
protest, protect, stand up for
justice, for our descendants legacy,
and for democratic principles–
may these colorful, heart-lifting,
light-bringing decorations
restore my resolve
for positive change to be done,
may this seasonal solstice
remind us the light can return
if we work together for the concepts
which will enhance lives globally–
whatever celebrations of light
people participate in...or not
I like to think my decorations express
my dream of an enlightened
perspective for a sustainable
and equitable world
in this one-sentence poem
wishing the best for everyone
this season and all others.

Mosaic Not Melting Pot

We become not a melting pot but a beautiful mosaic-different people, different beliefs, different yearnings, different hopes, different dreams. Jimmy Carter

Not a cauldron but a work of art-
different people color the pieces.
Different beliefs keep us apart.
Different yearnings, light - releases.
        Different hopes can make a quilt.
        Different dreams can be built.

Different people color the pieces,
can work together to create.
Understanding and hate decreases.
Encourage all to participate.
        We can connect, increase community.
        Treat all with respect, act with impunity.

Different beliefs keep us apart.
Sometimes it's hard to be tolerant.
Try to listen with the heart,
be sure you are not ignorant
        of positive, caring attitudes.
        Look for universal gratitudes.

Different yearnings, light-releases
can enhance creativity, problem-solving.
As cooperation increases,
we can see inequities dissolving.
        Yearnings can aim for the good of All.
        We need to learn the protocol.

Different hopes can make a quilt
to warm us, protect us from the cold.
Unleash our powers, toss out the guilt.
Think of the future, rethink the old.
        Mosaics can be made of sturdy stone.
        We can work together not alone.

Different dreams can be built,
the American dream seems diminished.
Re-dream with strengthened diverse conduit.
Make America great for all or dream vanished.
        A mosaic can rip apart at the seams.
        A melting pot boils and steams.

Clouded Mind

Moodlings

Heavy hearts
like heavy cloud in the sky,
are best relieved
by letting go
of a little water.

Christopher Morley

Asomatous

Having not material body; incorporeal. Dictionary.com

When the body aches and pains,
actions and projects go awry,
when moods and weather rains--
gosh, I wish I could fly!
       Bodiless like angels and sprites.
       Ah, the freedom! Oh, the delights!

Actions and projects go awry
when mind and limbs find limitations.
Just think in a blink of an eye
I could escape to other locations.
       Pure energy, conscious thought.
       No heaviness my body brought.

When moods and weather rains,
disincarnate I'd be impervious,
released from gravity's reins
and any conditions previous.
       I could be multi-dimensional.
       My efforts fully intentional.

Gosh, I wish I could fly--
to snuggle within a cloud,
travel throughout the galaxy,
do things not allowed
       in a fragile body, diminished mind.
       Multiversal access I could find.

Bodiless like angels and sprites,
changing density to suit situation.
Pick up a form to express insights
in a particular destination.
       A cosmic observer, above it all.
       All of creation at beck and call.

Ah, the freedom! Oh, the delights!
Un-tamped by lower level vibration.
Probably have to wait until final rites
to be free of this incarnation.
       How wonderful to be a spark
       to light up the deepening dark!

Sitting Out the Storm

A winter storm closes the Willamette Valley
snarling traffic and drivers in snow and ice.
Events, meetings, schools in the tally,
shallow-rooted trees, toppled in sacrifice.
   Everything's moving slower than Congress.
   I like the glisten on snow and ice, I confess.

Snarling traffic and drivers in snow and ice
storm laps like a wet tongue following the wind.
Stranded truckers, unchained cars paid price.
No gas or shelter could they find.
   The snow plows were very slow
   to reach the scene and let things go.

Events, meetings, schools in the tally.
Three gatherings cancelled I planned to attend.
Two meetings at my home failed to rally
poets afternoon or night out to contend
   with cold, plus slip and slide conditions.
   Warm indoors I escaped these renditions.

Shallow-rooted trees toppled in sacrifice.
An avalanche swallowed car on a mountain.
Crashes, downed power lines, flurries-- fluffy rice.
Standstills, engines want to move again.
   Hours trying to keep warm.
   Hours to be free from harm.

Everything's moving slower than Congress.
Husband took three times longer to get home.
He managed to get around some roadblocks--less
knowledgeable drivers had more dark hours to come.
   Think of all the vehicles in a traffic jam.
   Despite missed meetings–how lucky I am.

I like the glisten on snow and ice, I confess.
This morning I was able to sleep in.
No exercise class in this morning mess.
Chances for meetings here today are thin.
   So all the snacks are available to me.
   I'll continue my trek toward obesity.

Autumnal 2016

Red leaves inflame, fire flicks to the ground.
Autumn flames flash, flutter, shrivel and mound.
      Variations of reds vibrant this year.
      Tones of nation reddened, quaking in fear.
Serotinal sigh. Funereal sound.

Leaves of yellow, pink, red, tan, brown abound.
Fallen colors' diversity surround.
      Winter approaches with fate dolorous.
      Compost, recycle, renew these leaves and us.
Left swept up, while pick up problems compound.

Shadowing

The wishful thinking phrase "the shadows knows..."
The shadow knows what about anything?
Are shadows Rorschach Test shows
from 4th dimensional tinkering?
      Inkily blots cast on the ground.
      Do shadows resound sound?

The shadow knows what about anything?
Is it a blank black sheet, a negative?
What insights come from shadowing?
Foreshadowing projects a hint, what's intuitive?
      Near-noon I watched street-smudging trees
      dance on asphalt in choreographing breeze.

Are shadows Rorschach Test shows
for us to interpret like crop circles?
A film of darkness over what glows?
A shade-follower through our life cycles?
      Earth without shadows would be undone
      for if without shadows there's no sun.

From 4th dimensional tinkering–
shadows reflect control patterns of collective mind,
imprints from realm of 4D thinking?
Part of canopy form over sun body? Kind
      of a reminder of a sun patch,
      a blockage of light we can watch?

Inkily blots cast on the ground
wind-wiggle, sun-shift, earth-dance.
The diversity of silhouettes abound,
create an enchanting circumstance.
      Phantoms grovel underneath cars,
      only temporarily splaying charcoal scars.

Do shadows resound sound
like a CD disc or from the "cloud"?
What music or messages could be found
if our 3D consciousness allowed?
      Are shadows fuzzy pets? Our leaking dark selves?
      Specter-dopplegangers or from gloaming elves?

Rethinking the Holidays

We are about to celebrate Thanksgiving
based on Pilgrims dining with indigenous people.
We all know what happened after that feast.

This election year the popular vote didn't win.
I am hardly grateful for the injustice of this
and the aftermath of a unsuitable presidency.

Then comes Christmas--religious or secular--
divergent voices muted in the fiscal frenzy.
Santa dissed many wish lists this year.

Valentine's Day– harder to feel the love.
Easter- renewal of past antagonisms.
Fourth of July- What patriotism will be left?

Government holidays, Martin Luther King Jr.,
Veteran's Day, Memorial Day, Labor Day--
I am sure they are grumbling in their graves.

Perhaps we can mask our anger on Halloween.
Satiric costumes, replace reality with fantasy--
once again sugar up the children.

Holidays should be celebrations- joyous,
beacons of light in global dark times.
My mind and heart are just not into it this year.

What's Going On?

When I probe into the Cloud of Unknowing,
with organizational media manipulation,
evaluating concepts with glitches showing,
sorting out fact, theories, speculation--
>I have no firm view what's going on.
>What can I put my trust upon?

With organizational and media manipulation,
distortions and outright lies to sift through,
I ponder my puzzling situation
struggle to confirm a point of view.
>What might be considered fact changes.
>I consider what the update rearranges.

Evaluating concepts with glitches showing
causes me to discard ideas found wanting.
Pundits', politicians', pontiffs' words become mind-blowing--
out of touch, greedy, hierarchy flaunting
>power, controlling others' chances,
>creating inequitable circumstances.

Sorting out fact, theories, speculation
feeling skeptical, used, confused,
I wonder what is my obligation
to confront error, injustice, the abused.
>I research differing points of view, resources
>with little confidence in many discourses.

I have no firm view what's going on,
I see the cosmos through many lenses,
I question many answers held in common,
feel the inadequacies of my senses.
>Everything seems under constant test.
>I have to continue studying and do my best.

What can I put my trust upon--
some cosmic matrix, some prime creator?
What part do I play in this echelon?
A hologram, cosmic seed, soul innovator?
>Earth's an unharmonious place of conflicting choices,
>with a few limiting, manipulating many voices.

Showering Sound

On a summery day in the shower
the nozzle began to whine.
A glitch in the flow power?
Most of the time it was fine.
>I hold the head in different positions.
>Answers eluded with the transitions.

The nozzle began to whine
less of a hiss, more a meow.
The hose snaky scales began to shine,
but I conjure a silver cat tail now.
>When I turn the head a certain slant,
>the sound change was significant.

Most of the time it was fine.
Much like my life's flow.
Even in my aging decline
when my timing's a bit slow,
>I contemplate the scratchy sound
>itching my imagination around.

A glitch in the power flow?
Like me shifts in energy?
Down the drain the sounds go.
Raspiness remains with me.
>Another irritant unresolved.
>Another question unsolved.

Most of the time it was fine
to sit beneath the soulful spray.
I get my body to align
and let the bathing get underway.
>When the sound began to muzzle,
>I became distracted from the puzzle.

When my timing is a bit slow
and my arthritic knees throb,
I try to refocus, foreshadow
what is my next challenging job.
>Like write this poem in a new way--
>a variation of a trente-sei.

I hold the head in different positions.
Discover one angle makes it screech.
Maybe it's arthritic or leaky-- my suppositions,
ideas not totally out of reach.
>So I'll view the noise with compassion,
>perhaps it's following my wayward fashion.

Answers eluded with the transitions.
I step onto the mat. Water turned off.
I feel the pain of my conditions,
resume my allergy cough.
>Sneezing, wheezing I leave bathroom.
>What thoughts will now mushroom?

Do You Believe It?

If you believe it will work out, you'll see opportunities. If you believe it won't, you will see obstacles. Dr. Wayne D. Dyer

Whether I perceive opportunities or obstacles,
   I can't predict or consult oracles.
Sometimes it takes more than believing
    to heal the situation I'm relieving.

Sometimes obstacles and opportunities exist
    out of reach and persist.
Sometimes believing and receiving
    don't bring results; are deceiving.

Do I have informed enough perception
    to proceed with my selection?
I want to remain optimistic,
    but often that is not realistic.

Opportunities are seeds to bloom full.
    Obstacles are weeds to pull.
What I believe often does not matter.
    Both approaches can see dreams scatter.

Go Gentle Into a Dark Life

Doreen Virtue tries to heal trauma gently,
lift the clouds over our inner sparkle.
Try to view the world differently.
Brighten when we tend to darkle.
　　　　When you are feeling bruised blue,
　　　　sparkling can be hard to do.

Lift the clouds over our inner sparkle
seems heavy-lifting when weighed down.
What are the ways to re-sparkle?
Can you turn a rainbow frown upside down?
　　　　Clouds have rain and silver lining.
　　　　Depends on needs and what you're defining.

Try to see the world differently
avoid negative people, the news.
Try inspirational music and TV.
Pay attention to stressed body clues.
　　　　PTSD comes from many sources.
　　　　We must muster positive forces.

Brighten when we tend to darkle
can require an attitudinal overhaul.
Some people are toxic, hierarchal
put you down-- distance from them all.
　　　　Seek out the gentle folks
　　　　sharing loving strokes.

When you are feeling bruised blue,
stimulants seem an energizing idea.
I still like chocolate to see me through,
though not endorsed by P.C. media.
　　　　Caffeine, sugar also no-no.
　　　　Some things a diabetic should let go.

Sparkling can be hard to do.
Can we free our light from within
and let peaceful, happiness shine through?
Suffering tends to cloud, spin.
　　　　Can I avoid unstaged drama?
　　　　In the wings awaits trauma.

Dealing with Toxic People

Toxic people use fight, flight, freeze and fawn techniques. Doreen Virtue

You can respond with compassion,
        defuse friction.

Don't take actions personally.
        Actually

their problem. Take care of self–be
        free–sparkily.

Don't take abuse. Positively
role model. Can't fix or change them.
Support, sing Let it Go! Anthem.
Defuse friction. Actually free–sparkily.

On Guard

Oozing angst hardens into scars.
Drama/trauma seethes beneath the surface.
I'll distance myself from loved ones' wars,
hoping they'll do an about face.
   Memories intrude as nightmares.
   I continue to take on new cares.

Drama/trauma seethes beneath the surface.
I sense a volcano will erupt.
Their impacts I am unable to erase.
I know new fires will disrupt.
   I hold anxiety inside me
   even when they're not beside me.

I'll distance myself from loved one's wars
to keep some sense of hope and peace,
but I get drawn in again, reset high bars.
I wonder when I get to release
   some of the hurt they cause me.
   For my protection, I pause me.

Hoping they'll do an about face
without my comments, judgments, reports,
--let me build my own data base–
take their own initiative for supports.
   My heart and mind drain.
   I'm tired of carrying such pain.

Memories intrude as nightmares
whether day dreaming or at night.
My heart clams up as my mind prepares
to confront their latest plight.
   I'm left vulnerable when open
   when on guard for what can happen.

I continue to take on new cares
and some of their responsibilities.
Their actions toward others also wears.
I'm aware of their compromised abilities.
   I can't protect my fragmented soul
   as we all struggle to become whole.

101

Retaining Your Sparkle
Shine sparkly, light within, lift clouds and sparkle on. Doreen Virtue

Worldly trauma tends to darkle.
　　　Retain sparkle.

Use discernment with your contacts.
　　　Drama distracts.

Empower yourself. Use distance,
　　　few stimulants.

Can avoid hyper-vigilance.
Turn off toxic friendships and news.
Find inspiration, gentler views.
Retain sparkle. Drama distracts–few stimulants.

De-Stressing
   From Tips for De-Stressing from Doreen Virtue

If I am trying to de-stress–
lavender yes.

Essential oils also good.
Spray pillow–should.

Then play gentle music softly.
Get a CD.

Engage breathing in your belly,
yoga exercise. Belly dance?
Give daily de-stressing a chance–
lavender-yes, spray pillow-should, get a CD.

Scorched Wings

I want to remember that the grief threatened to carry me over the edge. I could not unfold my wings scorched from the cremation of my child into ash. The edge between madness and the ability to carry on, the dance between oblivion and love, feeling that one more day of such pain was impossible. And yet I walked step by step and took one more breath while my wings were repaired by the loving hands of friends and angels and my own determined self. Wendy Brown-Baez

For thirty-four years I've flown with singed wings,
after strewing the ashes of our son.
Whatever trauma the world brings,
I remember when I became undone.
       Shivering in shock, wings wrapped tight
       I cocooned, shuttered from dimmed light.

After strewing the ashes of our son,
barely functioning, I'd climbed the hill.
The path to recovery had begun.
The grief process burns me still.
       Friends and family prodded me on.
       I try not to focus on who is gone.

Whatever trauma the world brings
sends tremors of remembrance of his death.
I become a limp puppet with droopy strings,
seek angel uplifts underneath.
       Most days I relish any joys.
       Gifts perhaps of angelic ploys?

I remember when I became undone,
struggling to reassemble for commitments
to my family. I seek soul challenges to be won,
search for cosmic meaning, while earthly sentient.
       I wanted to know WHY?
       I give it my best multi-dimensional try.

Shivering in shock, wings wrapped tight–
unseen assistance helped me unfold.
My angel collection in clear sight,
up-vibed my spirits and behold–
       gradually I could smile and love
       with realms below and above.

I cocooned, shuttered from dimmed light.
My guardian angels must have observed
me bandaged, healing for flight,
saw my feathery needs served.
       I still fly with scorched wings,
       sputter for lift-off, repair flutterings.

A Good Life

A Good Life is not a place at which you arrive, it's a lens through which you see and create your world. Jonathan Fields

Pundits and gurus pontificate and preach
the principles of a good life in temple,
mosque, church--- revered dwellings, teach
through books and media- make it simple
      to create lists, guidelines to follow.
      What will concept theories allow?

The principles of a good life in temple
and sacred places present and past
try to give us an example
of ideas they hope will last.
      Similar discoveries lurk at their core.
      I see them, yet I am left wanting more.

Mosque, church, revered dwellings teach
the lens they wish you to perceive.
Religion expands control with outreach,
lay out benefits and dictums to believe.
      To each one's own if they don't impose
      their insights on those who oppose.

Through books and media-- make it simple.
Fields' 3 good life buckets, 5 human sparks.
Buckets of connection, vitality, contribution ample.
Sparks: mastery, curiosity, fascination embarks
      immersion and service into life and work.
      Integrate these concepts and don't shirk.

To create lists, guidelines to follow
are attempts to help others create a good life.
Our lenses determine how we see, hallow
our vision, hope to reduce our strife.
      But before we make any conversion
      determine if it is by choice, not coercion.

What will concept theories allow?
I keep my good life quest open-ended.
Plowing through fields, l leave most fallow.
On my inner instincts I've depended.
      I don't have answers or suggestions,
      but to be yourself, create own intentions.

Re-labeling Lit

When did I go from Chick Lit to Hen Lit?
Is this lit mostly prose written for women?
Mostly poets circle in my orbit.
When does slick chick become brooding hen?
  My preferred slant is feminist,
  with a playful cosmic twist.

Is this lit mostly prose written for women?
Hopefully not just romance and fantasy.
Women read and write broadly with acumen:
science, spirituality, philosophy, mystery.
  Poetry is my favorite genre, its true,
  but I've lots of prose research to probe into.

Mostly poets circle in my orbit.
They're both grounded and lift cosmically,
write widely, seriously and with wit,
try to express their reality creatively.
  Prose sentences clog heavier as I age.
  With poetic lines it's quicker to turn page.

When does slick chick become brooding hen?
I dislike both terms for feminine gender.
I prefer girl, We Moon, or womyn.
And then there is transgender.
  Despite a few differing parts,
  all sexes can have loving hearts.

My preferred slant is feminist.
I like to open opportunities and empower.
I want hierarchies to get the gist,
there is only equal not higher or lower.
  Despite labels, we must liberate
  people to fulfill dreams and create.

With a playful, cosmic twist
I want to explore the whole universe.
I'd be an eternal reincarnationalist
so I could examine the mulitiverse.
  Wherever my location or whatever my form,
  I seek peace and freedom to be the norm.

Defining Poetry

All the lines start with a capital letter and don't reach the other side of the page.
Definition of poetry by five year old girl.

When I was six, I dictated rhymed quatrains.
My mother wrote my lines. I could not read.
I moved on from rhymes and refrains,
whatever my later poems need.
> I've practiced over 1000 different forms.
> I delight to see how a poem transforms.

My mother wrote my lines I could not read.
I could see how my words patterned the page.
Diverse designs with rules to heed,
help my ardent ideas to engage.
> My line lengths can sprawl across a sheet–
> terse or rambling–or prose poem feat.

I moved on from rhymes and refrains,
to free verse, spoken word, many concoctions,
ignoring boundaries, thought that restrains.
I like to fully explore my diverse options.
> I'll create a new form if old one won't do.
> It is the poetically correct thing to re-view.

Whatever my later poems need
when editing or in throes of creation,
I don't want anything to impede
my current poem's inspiration.
> I welcome poems as a delight
> even in the middle of the night.

I've practiced over 1000 different forms
and word-played many thousands of poems.
Poems to cause reflection or inform,
many moods, protests and anthems.
> No matter the intent of my words,
> I hope they keep coming in herds.

I delight to see how a poem transforms
from a glint, a spark, to ignite flame.
Light perseveres through storms.
Fun to see how wildfire tames.
> Poems defy definition. I'll be terse.
> A life without poetry would be much worse.

True to Form

Life, with its rules, its obligations, and its freedoms, is like a sonnet: You're given the form, but you have to write the sonnet yourself. Madeleine L' Engle

My sonnet would challenge the rules and obligations.
I want to know what say I had in coming to this world.
Guidelines and freedoms differ in all nations.
Much of the best of life, to many, remains unfurled.

We are given a form? By whom? We fill in blanks?
What part do we play in any cosmic plan?
What if we find thanks and soon life tanks?
Do we go back, hurl forward, erase ban?

Our bodies manifest our myriad sentience.
Is the goal being kind, service, love, light?
Do we create lives with help of guided conscience?
Will we ever get rules and obligations right?

Life has AAHS, ahas, oh-ohs, oh-nos,
Maybe I'm supposed to write in prose.
    Maybe not write life- just live it.

Beauty in Poetry
The only reality is Beauty and Its only perfect expression is Poetry. Stephane Mallarme

Poetry's perfect expression?
Beauty's only reality?
Maybe it is delusional?
Not all's beautiful or perfect?

Maybe in another dimension
poetry's perfect expression?
Poet's express more than beauty.
Our reality dims darkly.

Beauty is a joy forever
poets dream and all writers hope.
Poetry's perfect expression?
Other perspectives might contest.

Poetry, beauty sound lofty–
not grounded to Earth's perception.
Somewhere viewed from clouds maybe–
poetry's perfect expression?

Killer Poetry

I doubt writing poetry would save any species.
We even kill the one animal that does poeticize.
If poetry doesn't decide which animals survive,
what is our criteria for who lives or dies?

Religion saves sacred cows in some cultures.
Some people do not eat animals at all.
Some animals just don't appeal or taste that good.
People can follow war rules and slaughter protocol.

We can wax poetic over some creatures,
write requiems when they go extinct,
compose protest poems to protect them,
but poetry won't save many critters, I think.

Whether animals are humble or snooty,
to respect all beings is poetry's duty?

Beclouded

Attempts at Healing

I think you should aim
for the stars—
and hopefully avoid
ending up in the clouds.

Roxanne McKee

Odd Ode to My Knees

My arthritic knees need encouragement,
praise for their efforts to support
a rickety, heavy weight, bone-on-bone crone.

When I travel to the East Coast or Sweden,
I numb inflammation with cortisone,
so they can enjoy the journey as well.

I give them respite with walkers or wheelchairs.
They bask in breeze– the bee's knees,
vacationing from strain and pain.

I pamper them with acupuncture, massage, pills,
physical therapy, bojo balls, balms and creams,
crystals, "goose juice", heat/cold, prayer, meditation.

My masseuse trims my toenails with her clippers
so my knees do not have to contort, bend awkwardly
or ungracefully beyond their tolerance and stretch.

Dark chocolate elevates their mood if not position,
soothed by sweetness, each bite a break
and a jolt of energy for the next step.

A meditative CD supposedly heals my knees
by sound and colors, reaching my third eye which monitors
progress toward greater mobility and comfort.

I will my knees the essence of the slow-stepper, tardigrade-
indestructible, adapter under all conditions,
be capable of dancing in fubsy form?

Knees, thank you for your patience with an impatient patient.
Together, cosmos willing we will go far.
My hopes are riding, writing on you.

Walkers

When the legs are weak and need support
I turn to mechanical and human walkers.
My husband pushes a wheelchair–good sport.
Two metallic walkers cause gawkers.
>   I need to balance and sit.
>   With walkers I make the best of it.

I turn to mechanical and human walkers
as canes make me feel unstable.
Insectoid designs make excellent stalkers,
get me in places I'm not usually able.
>   Hunched over grips one walker has seat-one a tray
>   I can pause, carry items, accessorized on my way.

My husband pushes a wheelchair–good sport
to lug my luggish lard, for its often hard
to challenge uneven terrain of a tricky sort.
He's my access and my sturdy body guard.
>   Museums, festivals and fairs are the longest places,
>   he grips handle bars for unpredictable interfaces.

Two metallic walkers cause gawkers
as inside a gray tray carries my foods,
let's me gather with other talkers,
outside I have a seat to store goods.
>   I hide my purse, writing supplies,
>   carefully tread, my cautious tries.

I need to balance and sit
when legs tire. Walkers provide knee relief.
Carrying remotes, weights, exercise bands a prime benefit.
Walkers expand horizons is my belief.
>   My tools travel with me wherever I go.
>   I'm not in a standstill. I can flow.

With walkers I make the best of it.
I want to add colorful tapes, maybe a trinket
to dangle or swirl around, maybe spin it.
All I have to do is conjure and think it.
>   What fun to walk with ribbons and baubles draping.
>   An artsy, practical project I'm partaking.

Needling Pincushion

I am a fleshy pincushion
shot full of holes.
Daily insulin injections.
>Bi-weekly acupuncture
>Monthly B-12 shots.
>Occasional blood draws.
>Not enough diabetes testing.
>Now series of three, both knee shots
>added to earlier knee cortisone injections.
>Now a flu shot on the other arm from B-12.

Bandages to peel.
Bruises to fade.
Pain to forget.
Punctures to heal.

As needles penetrate my skin
putting liquids into my body
for health purposes--
I prefer a pill method.

Unlike a non-fleshy pin cushion
my needles do not stick around.
Walking about like a porcupine
might make dressing difficult.

As I expose vulnerable areas
to get poked, mostly with cleansing,
and antibiotic swipes, I hope
this fleshy pin cushion stops bleeding.

I can deal with temporary discomfort.
Pin cushions hold tools to create
the fabric of something new.
I am patterning polka dots.

Testing Obstacles

My doctor's appointment is 8:30.
Check-in at 8:15. Labs beforehand.
Great because I was fasting. But...
the blood-suckers have poor aim, I face bruising.

I went the previous Friday morning,
but the lab had not received the doctor's orders.
So I went home and ate,
relieved to escape being a pincushion.

A few hours later the lab orders came through,
but I had eaten by then, broken fast,
so had to come in before the appointment.
A weekend before being punctured with needles.

Dutifully, warily, I reported for blood tests.
Blood shots were off target. I left with five cotton balls taped
to both elbow creases and right hand.
Then I was informed I needed a urine test.

Of course, I had fasted, tried to clear out systems.
No water to prime. Now dehydrated,
lots of blood-letting as well.
I saw doctor dry, bloodied and puff-balled.

I needed to drink water and report
back to the lab for the urine test.
Still fasting and thirsty, I read magazines
to distract myself until systems ready to go.

Finally I headed to the cubicle
small cup in hand wondering
if I could ever aim the small stream.
Usually a problem even when prepared.

A kind lab tech gave me a white, plastic
cowboy hat to invert on the toilet seat.
It would catch every smidgeon of moisture,
to drain into the cup. Good to the very last drop.

With the glitches in the test procedures,
it would be days before results came in.
Like a tagged animal I awaited the doctor's call
so he could proclaim – carry on as is.

I'm a golf course full of holes --
bandaged from a B-12 shot as well.
The nurse plopped the only shot
that was a hole in one.

Bringing Home the Bacon

Stymied by many attempts
to reduce inflammation from
arthritic bone on bone knees,
the shaman proclaimed "bacon".

He intuited I should try putting bacon
on my knees- two strips and see
what happens. My knees get creamed,
tried magnets, crystals, boji balls.

Why not bacon? It could be a miracle cure.
If it does not work for healing,
I enjoy eating crispy bacon,
though not supposed to.

At the supermarket I find bacon.
All kinds, all prices. Some on sale.
Hickory flavored- so if test fails,
I'll enjoy pigging out.

He says I can reuse the strips
if refrigerated, but don't eat test strips.
It's probably like acupuncture
releasing toxins-- pain-piercing bacon.

It is an experiment so I do not know
how long to sit here at the computer
with both knees taped with bacon.
Bacon smells better cooked.

Will body heat start to cook the strips?
The phone rings. I grasp the strips in one hand,
walk over to the phone, holding it in the other.
I don't explain to my grandson what I am doing.

Back to the computer, I reapply
the strips to my slimy knees.
Soon I must think about lunch.
I have lost my appetite for bacon.

I do not know how many hours or days
I should apply bacon to my porcine body.
Maybe I'll just bring home the bacon
for frying in a pan. I hope for healing.

Napping with Bacon

When I went from my computer to nap
I did not take a book by the literary Bacon
or a fleshy form of someone of the same name,
but pale, striped, strips of raw bacon dripping,
dangling awkwardly from my knees.

It is day one of the bacon test
to see if bacon strips will reduce pain
from my pain-in-the-knees. I stand
hunched to hold the center of the crosses
of the bacon strips, hobble to the couch.

Sun streams in the window as I place
my knees on a pillow, arrange the bacon
and hope the sun does not cook them.
I hood my face to keep me from skin cancer.
Sunrays across my belly and breast.

The phone only rings once—a scam
wanting to disrupt my ham. I do not
rise for it. My husband asks me to
autograph my latest book for a friend.
I do so- without moving my legs.

After a rest, now several hours with bacon,
I get up, fistful of slime, wrap it in foil for tomorrow,
head to the bathroom where I wash off
my hands and knees with Irish Spring soap
so my scent does not attract bugs, repel people.

Back at the computer I record the test results.
Not much change I can see, but then
the grease on my skin might moisten it.
Tonight watching Dancing With the Stars,
I'll know I'm not dancing yet... when pigs can fly.

Bacon Test #2

After an afternoon class teaching
I was ready to lift up my legs and nap.
It was a warm day, but our home, cool.
The sun did not directly hit the couch.

I went to the fridge to get the foil-wrapped
recycled bacon strips My baggy pants were
easy to roll up, I plunked on the couch,
opened the foil to bacon-bandage my knees.

Four cold strips made two crosses
not a red cross but pink and white
like a candy stripper. Less slippery,
smelly, and less clingy than yesterday.

This test was an hour and a half.
One hour I was asleep. Half-hour
trying to sleep as my husband
chatted on the phone nearby.

Breakfast we ate out so I had bacon,
ate out lunch as well so well-fueled.
Knees medicated with cream,
two Aleve, still throbbed and painful.

When I first rested, the extra-banged up
right knee complained more, felt heated.
But after the bacon application as skin
greases, in a few minutes, calmed.

Whether rest or bacon, when I washed
the knees and walked to the computer
both knees had not rived up as much.
I wrapped and refrigerated test bacon strips.

Uncooked, unrecycled bacon
lay like languishing tongues,
reminded me of crisp breakfast bacon.
How many test strips do I need?

Bacon Test #3

Test #3 was conducted sitting
in a rocking chair in front of TV.
I draped the knees in the two crosses,
had a supper salad to nibble.

This was a two hour test.
One-half hour of Jeopardy,
One-half hour of Big Bang Theory.
One hour PBS documentary on diabetes.

A lone moth circled and witnessed
this bacon test, but not with close scrutiny.
I washed my slime with fragrant soap,
went to the kitchen to return dish.

I decided since my knees did feel
less inflamed, I would cut two bacon
slices into four strips and cook them.
Bacon inside might double results.

While bacon cooked, I researched
gut bacteria: Firmicuties---fat-builders
and Bacteroidetes– fat-burners.
I need the latter after eating bacon.

When I turned over the burnt-edged bacon
they had shrunk into four morsels, barely
a mouthful. Humm...should I cut two more
strips or save them for further bacon tests?

Bacon Test #4

Today's test is a time management problem.
In the morning I have exercise class,
afternoon Cooperative Scrabble and
evening poetry class meets here.

Best timing is 11-2 with lunch break
which was time set aside for writing
daily April Poem-A-Day challenge. So
I sit at computer with bacon-crossed knees.

This is the last day of recycled bacon strips.
I am alone to deal with odor and can wash
before guests arrive at my home.
These strips are cold and still knee bend.

I will try one and one-half hours, no
snacking, no moving from the office chair.
It does not rock, but tolerates some movement.
My knees warm the bacon greasy.

I should assess if I am getting results
other than cold packs would. Bacon
perhaps has salt or some ingredient
that soothes inflammation, softens skin?

I am not sure the idea of bacon bandages
is the band-aid of choice. Like rocks, crystals,
magnets they tie you down. Creams
and pills easier to incorporate into my day.

Last night after I burned two bacon strips
cut into four pieces, then left two strips
long, but not cooked to very crispy, I
kind of lost my hankering for ham.

I have one more package of bacon
since it was a sale. Will it be dedicated
to research or culinary chance? If
I turn on space heater, will they cook?

The Energetic Hitch-hiker

Sitting on facing chairs, the shaman and I
were doing sound healing with brass bowls,
when the shaman noticed a spirit being
watching us from a nearby chair.

The shaman paused and described
an ephemeral form dressed
rather sparkly and garishly.
Not a classic angel type.

The shaman could not determine
gender which I said did not matter.
I just wondered what this unseen energy
wanted with me. What was its purpose?

The shaman asked if I know its name.
I said no, maybe cosmic chum?
This made the entity chuckle
and said that was fine.

When I asked if it brought recent nightmares,
it said yes to get my attention.
Then I became suspicious and asked why
would a good-intentioned spirit do that?

Did the spirit wake me up the previous night
about three and not let me go back to sleep
until I had a rough draft of a trente-sei?
The unnamed spirit laughed yes. For me poor timing.

The shaman consulted my higher self for clarity
as he was skeptical of these intentions also.
Despite the spirit's claims it was here with sparks of humor
for my highest good, a higher honcho swished it away.

The shaman said the spirit was with me about ten days,
energetically hitch-hiking on my light.
A surprising, more positive placement would arrive
in about a week to help me with my poetry.

Metaphysically I've read about all kinds
of drop-ins, walk-ins, soul-exchanges, ghosts,
diverse light and dark multi-dimensional beings.
I wish I could spot dark ones myself–blow them away.

Healing Alliance

Nightly, I high-jump onto my lofty bed
    rearrange pillows for my head and under my knees.
        After I place my pillow props, flake my arms
           on the quilt or under it if chilled,
              I turn off the light.

The monotone meditation tape drones, guru urges me
    to make myself comfortable, close my eyes,
        breathe deeply and relax, listen to the music
           of some exotic instrument, breathe
              for a healthier state of mind.

I find a position I can remain in for awhile,
    pay attention to patterns, color codes encoding healing,
        notice the subtle changes in wordless musical score.
           The contrast of flat voice and twanging tones
              bores or hypnotizes me.

Then I'll absorb color vibrations my inner body knows will dance
    with consciousness in a kaleidoscopic experience.
        Sound and color sensations flow through me, resonate,
           opening the body to higher consciousness
              for health, well-being and balance.

All this vibrating, inhaling, relaxing, deep breathing
    supposedly cleanses organs and functions,
        gently dissolves and releases blockages.
           I am bathed in light and sound,
              wait for beneficial effects of frequencies.

Red, orange, yellow, green, light blue, indigo, violet, white
    chakra colors come and go. In the flow until I glow,
        entering mind, body and spirit to heal
           in a higher state of consciousness,
              clearer state of being...hopefully.

Or until I fall asleep, often after blue– my favorite color.
    If I stay awake to the end, open my eyes, I know
        I am in for a long, dark night in this painful dimension–
           not the dream dimension where there is a possibility
              my muse or angelic guides might heal me.

Cloudscapes

Quirks

Our mind is like a cloudy sky;
in essence clear and pure,
but overcast by clouds of delusions.
Just as the thickest clouds
can disperse,
so too,
even the heaviest delusions
can be removed
from our minds.

Kelsang Gyatso

March, 1940

I go back to my pre-birth,
try to justify accepting this assignment
to Earth, 1940.

Was this to be another hoped for growth spurt?
Atonement for some previous karmic debt?
Was this upcoming life the best selection?

Was I forced to follow a pattern
in some cosmic plan or given
some creative license, personal input?

I've read we do create a life chart
with some free will, but some challenges.
We chose parents, time and location.

Intuitives told me I did accept this assignment,
but with some reluctance because Earth
was not a favorite landing due to past experiences.

So why did I come? For the Love? To help?
To learn? To teach? To repair past relationships?
On non-optimistic days, I wish I went elsewhere.

Subconsciously I yearn for other dimensions.
I dream next time I can go to a place
of peace, light, love, positive connections.

But in March 1940, I chose a mixed bag.
Overall, I have experienced much joy
as a troubled world appears to crumble around me.

Indigo Blues

Cosmic, caring Indigo children are natural children in an unnatural world. Believed to possess unusual supernatural traits, paranormal abilities, telepathy, more empathetic and creative, strong-willed and curious travelers between worlds at night.

I think I met an authentic Indigo,
a starseed awakening to his mission,
perhaps a third rock star like Ringo
waiting for his cosmic commission.
      Do Indigos have enhanced DNA?
      Will they bring a Golden Age some day?

A starseed awakening to his mission,
he has the symptoms, has done research.
He's hoping for some guiding transmission
for more answers from his search.
      Is he part of fifth dimensional shift
      or part of humanity's global uplift?

Perhaps a third rock star like Ringo
tuning us into the music of the spheres,
connecting Earthlings to cosmos – bingo
greater planetary understanding appears?
      Is this all some New Age fantasy?
      Part of a multiversal mystery?

Waiting for his cosmic commission
he prepares to be ready to bring light.
He yearns to receive permission,
to perform his roles, make things bright.
      (Maybe this sounds surreal,
      but I hope it becomes real.)

Do Indigos have enhanced DNA?
Twelve strands to our two?
Are they capable of higher realm tasks
most older people cannot do?
      Will their children be Crystals
      with all the gifts prophesy foretells?

Will they bring a Golden Age someday?
Such luminous clarity, wonderful dreams!
Meanwhile we can live in a harmonic way,
so the future can be better than it seems.
      May guides enlighten this Indigo youth,
      so he can find and share universal truth.

How to Get To My House

First do not come to my house if you are
        allergic to dust
        claustrophobic
        lack a sense of humor or whimsy
        bringing indoor pets, especially cats.

If you do not have a GPS proceed north
        on Ninth St. One street north of Walnut
        to Hemlock, turn left when you spy 7/11.

When you see a green house
        with gray trim, chosen by my husband
        to reflect Oregon's green and fog,
        open the airlock door.

Thousands of angels will swarm around you
        dangle from the ceiling, sprawl shelves, tabletops.
        Seasonal decorations crowd all surfaces.
        The mini-museum creatures stare at you,
        hope you'll feel welcome and not sneeze.

Prepare for inanimate peekers in the bathroom.
        Be aware some decorations are out of season.
        Some annuals have become perennials.
        Enjoy the snacks, Swedish toarpskronen,
        wooden angels, Swedish folk figures in dining room.

Do not enter into my office called the Grand Canyon.
        Files and books cover the wooden walls.
        The center stores more books and paperwork.
        Projects engulf crowded computer nook.

Every room has lots of art, color, miniatures,
        places for visitors, writers, Scrabble players
        to dine and play. Always something to look at.

Some people see only clutter. I see joyful muses.
        When you get to my house, expect surprises.
        If you don't come in, the yard art wild animals
        parading under the front windows
        will wave their tails good-bye.

Antennae

Somewhere something incredible is waiting to be known. Carl Sagan

We search within and without to learn.
The unseen and seen exude energy.
Moving animates we believe are alive.
Maybe different levels of sentience
and vibrations of particles
also exist in what we consider inanimate.

When I look at my miniature collections,
created by machines and by human hands,
I view them as antennae to draw creative energy,
to ground the expressions of artistic beings.
They might not be considered great art,
but their gathering of color and joy
make them antennae wherever they surface.

Polka-dots of color on shelves and tables,
in concealed doll houses where they could exude
an essence we cannot perceive.
Perhaps sculpture and paintings
also lure our curiosity and energize our spirits.

Antennae send or receive electromagnetic waves.
All is energy. Who is to say what gets to wave?
Antennae possibilities could be anywhere
in everything besides us.
Makes you want to treat everything
with kindness and respect.
Never know where we flow
and how the receiver might react.

Whigmaleeries

A whim, notion. Whimsical or fanciful ornament or contrivance. Gimmick.

My home is a mini-museum of whigmaleeries:
creatures of imagination in whimsical forms,
collections of owls, angels, elves, and fairies,
dressed in fanciful and surreal uniforms.
> Yard art parades under our front windows.
> Swedish folk art and figures appear as holiday allows.

Creatures of imagination in whimsical forms
line shelves, counters, coffee tables, dangle in air.
Each creature clusters, groups with own norms.
Each entity can see in case it is aware.
> Inanimates might animate internal energy,
> chat on a wave-length we can't perceive.

Collections of owls, angels, elves and fairies
indicate my penchant for beings with wings.
I host thousands of winged imaginaries,
along with dolls, grounded folk-artsy things.
> Two enchanting dollhouses with multiple floors,
> my parents made for doll families to explore.

Dressed in fanciful and surreal uniforms
they mask their essence, put on an engaging show.
They're perched in their places in gathered swarms.
Each gets a viewpoint and companions to know.
> Endearing whimsy in their faces and costume,
> bring joy to me and others I assume.

Yard art parades under our front windows
strides sidewalk chunks, shines in the sun.
Snails, birds, pig, turtle, hedgehog spirit glows.
Our search for fanciful wild animals is not done.
> A butterfly whirligig spins in the wind.
> I'm eager to know what other wildlings we'll find.

Swedish folk art and figures appear as holiday allows,
strut their stuff, decorate special occasions.
Some displays overlap as my aging slows
my seasonal exchanges and my new inspirations.
> Perennial or seasonal creatures always surround me.
> Inspirited miniatures lift me to fly and ground me.

Halloween In August

Each season brings some holiday to celebrate.
Boxes and storage bins stack in my closet.
Creatures and symbols wait to emerge
from plastic mummy wraps, free from hibernation.

Decorations have varying durations.
I tend to overlap. Christmas can stay present
in the enclosed outdoor room for years.
Inside Christmas remains to merge with other shifts.

I tend to think Halloween gets short shrift
if it does not get a head start. Thanksgiving
gets squished between it and Christmas.
So I am putting away Fourth of July.

Family and friends think I am nuts
to pre-season fall in the midst of balmy summer.
Perhaps the witches and warlocks are overdressed,
they are mostly stuffed felt creatures by Annalie.

For over 50 years I have collected celebratory figures.
Seasonal displays change in some areas
and are perennials in others. Halloween
is a seasonal variety. I love their spark.

I decorate two coffee tables in the living room
after removing marching mice and people
in red-white and blue– a top hat dog on a donkey
waving instruments, kites, hats, hot dogs, baskets.

Now grinning pumpkins, costumes, parade.
Orange, black, purples predominate.
Then on the buffet my coven of whimsical witches.
I smile at their perky poses and puckish faces.

Two bathrooms: one hosts black cats
and mice dressed in witchy garb.
The other shows fascinating youthful witches.
Toilet top specializes in gray-haired crones.

Room to room my miniatures enchant me
They never cease to catch my eye and heart.
Their upbeat vibes, quirky essence uplift me.
I wander in my mini-museum gathering joy.

De-stuffing

My home is a de-cluttering pro's nightmare.
There are people who can set up an estate sale.
These folks are orderly, acutely aware,
figuring out prices and each detail.
       Hopefully I'll leave things here until I'm dead
       or they could fill a storage area instead.

There are people who can set up an estate sale
for anything they think will sell.
I'd leave instructions for some recipients to prevail,
to follow our trust's requests. Who can tell
       what will happen is beyond knowing.
       No need for any of it where I'm going.

These folks are orderly, acutely aware,
of the value of things, what my bequests are.
Hopefully they'll be fair and square.
Will I be watching from questing star?
       My plan is to enjoy my possession now.
       Don't worry too much about tomorrow.

Figuring out prices and each detail
will present an enormous challenge, patience.
I don't have time or math to use sliding scale,
recycle my goods, display charity, resilience.
       My son would make it dumpster trash.
       Would he feel his mother's backlash?

Hopefully I'll leave things here until I'm dead.
I donate, gift, but re-stuff once more.
I'll be a guardian, care-taker instead?
There is so much art, many media to explore.
       My home reflects my identity,
       a place to express creativity.

Or they could fill a storage area instead.
It would take pressure off landfills.
A flummoxed pro shakes flustered head
or relative recycles or maybe even thrills.
       A future archeologist's de-cluttering role
       worsens in case of an earthquake or sinkhole.

Downsizing

My peer-group has been downsizing--
de-stuffing, donating, moving their junk.
With less mobility and senility it's not surprising,
waiting for the wheelchair and a new part kerplunk.
>I live in a cluttered, mini-museum menagerie.
>I can't imagine sorting, discarding this debris.

De-stuffing, donating, moving their junk,
they sift through memories, what they'll need.
They huff and puff then hire a hunk.
It is an anxiety-ridden situation, indeed.
>How much storage in their new place?
>It feels like a desperate time chase.

With less mobility and senility it's not surprising
since mind and body work deficiently.
Their world closes down, fear's rising.
They need changes to act efficiently.
>Some make downsizing decisions and consent
>to letting others do caring and chores they resent.

Waiting for the wheelchair and a new part kerplunk
requires diligence and bodily focus.
Sadly your circumference has shrunk.
You know there is no hocus-pocus.
>But if your mind is not clear
>you'll forget what you held dear.

I live in a cluttered, mini-museum menagerie
thousands of angels and seasonal collections.
Every surface and wall covered–little space free
of my recording, hoarding, recollections, selections.
>Color and texture sparkle my eye.
>Downsize? I won't even try.

I can't imagine sorting, discarding this debris.
Some possessions designated, but otherwise--
those who'd enjoy them- I'd gift them lovingly.
When I'm demented, disabled, someone else can downsize.
>I use walker and wheelchair–I'm on my way
>to becoming downsized any dizzy-downed day.

Cleaning House...and Senate

My husband insists on vacuuming
with an ort-snorting, bulbous triceratops,
the long-nosed, elephantine Miele–
like a stubborn Democrat
lugging a recalcitrant Republican
into cleaning up its act.

I refuse to use the snuffling creature,
with tripping tentacle cords,
bumptious behavior,
heavy, clumsy reminder
of a dirtied reality
I am resistant to confront.

When we had an upright cleaner
it could function as a cane–
an aid to stability, but
the Hoover snout crumped out.
Then hubby took over with his vacuum choice.
When he quits, someone else will clean-sweep.

My Unzippered Coat

For several years my blue, soft coat
slumped on a Shaker knob in the hall.
Somehow the zipper stuck at the bottom.
It would not budge, no matter how hard I tried.

None of my other coats was as comfortable,
such a lovely light shade of sky blue.
The fleece once cuddled me warm.
Now it hung as a droopy cloud.

The day was a perfect day for the coat.
I decided to take it to the cleaners,
so the seamstress could put in a new zipper.
If I could not wear it today–maybe another day.

The seamstress deftly tugged and pulled,
nudging the zipper to release its grip.
Voila! It opened and zipped to the top.
I did not need a new zipper.

We tried several times to see if it was
indeed unstuck and not about to click shut.
I put on the coat on this serendipitous day,
high collar warming my neck. Body bulging it.

I thanked her and asked the fixing fee.
She smiled and said I owed her nothing.
She had not had to replace the zipper,
it was only stuck and she freed it.

If there was any dust from hanging around
so long on a hook, it dispersed into balmy air.
The coat billowed cumulous. I hugged the blues away.
We floated together– bluing the sky.

To Do List When Traveling East

1. Relax and pack luggage leisurely.

2. Try not to panic about getting to airport on time.
   Tamp anxiety. Store dark chocolate.

3. Do not get frantic about traffic, getting luggage, myself
   plus wheelchair to boarding pass station. Be zen.

4. Don't stare at the cultural, digital and fashion diversity.
   Enjoy overhearing conversations.

5. Remain calm in the cramped seat and to the screech
   of two children behind me. Get earplugs?

6. Focus on telling my body I am on East coast time
   and the red-eye flight is just a sleepless night.

7. Tell achy muscles and weary brain, pain relief
   is just a cup of water away.

8. Tell your heart you are prepared to handle
   the emotional changes since you've been away.

9. Greet your home state's history with openness.

10. The autumn leaves are turning, you are returning
    to watch and catch their fall.

The Fit is not Fit

Our new blue Fit is not fit.
It had a breakdown in a Safeway gas station.
Kind of left us in a snit.
We did not reach our destination.
      In a drizzly rain shower
      we had to wait an hour.

It had a breakdown in a Safeway gas station.
Out of town it would not start or shift gears.
We called insurance in the expectation
we'd wait until a tow truck appears.
      Husband's cell called and put him through paces-
      sometimes by computer, or with unseen faces.

Kind of left us in a snit.
We had to call and cancel several plans.
We squished three in super duty, tow truck to sit
and follow caravans of sedans.
      Driver kindly dropped us at home.
      Left Fit at repair shop. Fit can't roam.

We did not reach our destination
a visit with friends and a poetry reading.
We filled out paperwork, left keys in anticipation
the Fit would get next day care it's needing.
      Since Fit would not take us afar,
      we'd rely on our hybrid car.

In a drizzly rain shower,
we'd huddled in car under a overhang.
Fit would not run under own power.
So we talked, waiting for what call brang.
      Our plans required a revision.
      We made another decision.

We had to wait an hour
for deliverance. Meanwhile our deliberation
provided husband a swim, me a nap;
later dinner with grandson. When back in operation--
      because battery cell died, recharged next day,
      fixed unfit Fit now flits on its way.

Viewing the Three Sisters

I watch from the car
snow-capped mountains blur by,
majestic views seen from afar.
Even under blue, cloudless, summer sky
they fly-by fast.
My head turns to follow.
Such pure grandeur, magic can't last.
My vision mists. Happy tears won't allow
seeing with clarity–
Faith, Hope and Charity.

Re-sourcing

Leaning on the shopping cart to relieve knee pressure
I troll the aisles, plucking produce and products.
The 15-item check-out is my usual exit.
Absentmindedly, I unload my groceries on the conveyor.

An old man with a walker in his cart
is behind me with about five items.
I knew if he had a walker, he shared sore legs.
He would not want to wait for my bulky, buying binge.

I told the clerk to take him before me.
She was not her customer-cheery self.
She planned a break after me.
I'd delayed her as well.

After she processed my 24 items,
she made a hasty retreat, barely giving
me my Monopoly pieces (for grandson)
and sales slip with number for customer service.

My knees were stinging as I boarded my cloth bags
in the back of my beloved blue Fit, grateful to sit
before I belted up and pressed a button to go.
A crow bobbed after lean-picking pavement litter beside me.

The crow and I paused and acknowledged each other.
We are all feeding on the same resources.
Transients, we both leave the darkled parking lot
without second-hand goods. Hungry.

The Blueberry Battle

When I open the refrigerator
the plastic jaws of the blueberry container
snap open like an alligator's maw
and splatter blueberries
all over the kitchen floor
in a pattern like a particle collision at CERN.

I was really looking forward
to organic blueberries in my yogurt.
At first I stare at the blue dots
sprawling, radiating widely
on the brown, marbled bamboo floor.
Then I ponder how to gather them up.

I decide on a dustpan and broom.
Awkwardly I chase the blue balls
spilling out of the pan as much as in.
I swat them in and they roll out.
The ones I catch I plop in a strainer.
I sweep up other detritus as well.

Who knew all the dried grass, mud chips, stems,
pills, paper scraps huddling with the blueberries.
It took quite a while to corral all the debris.
After washing them in the strainer
I hand-pick each shiny, wet berry
and put the blue orts in a bowl.

The gunky- junk leftovers I dump in the trash,
rinse the strainer and leave it to dry.
I have blueberry squish marks on the floor
and on my fingers to clean. Finally when I plunk
the chosen ones to bubble in my yogurt,
battle fatigue sets in with breakfast mood blues.

I'm Not Into Pet Control

I am not a pet controller or owner.
This is my fervent, personal choice.
My friends' accounts make me a pet-groaner.
My abstinent stance needs a voice.
>>At exercise class each animal lover regales
>>the antics, the costs each pet entails.

This is my fervent, personal choice
to remain people-centric, pet free.
Actually I can listen and rejoice,
I am relieved and regret free.
>>I don't want to control any creature.
>>Domestic pets require this feature.

My friends' accounts make me a pet-groaner
when cats' and dogs' acts are not so lovable.
Guardians complain of mischief, become a moaner
over the losses, not recoverable.
>>When pets die, they are bereft–
>>grieving, uncomforted, lonely, left.

My abstinent stance needs a voice.
I don't want lickings, cuddlings from a pet.
I don't miss expensive vet invoice
from the latest malady–and yet
>>though I don't want pet responsibility
>>I can understand need for companionability.

At exercise class each animal lover regales
cute and clever incidents, how they cherish
the love pets bring to their lives and tales
of efforts they make so pets flourish.
>>Good-bye to an ornamented Christmas tree.
>>Put things away. Keep home hazard free.

The antics, the cost each pet entails
are recounted with delight, sometimes worry.
We are privy to all the pets' private details.
I am not convinced. I am not sorry.
>>I like my home danderless, pet excrement-less.
>>Let me make my own household mess.

Yard Art

We are creating a patio for yard art,
underneath our two front windows.
We put in sidewalk chunks, tore bushes apart,
more like a walkway than familiar patios.
        We want to line the pathway with pizzaz
        like our inside mini-museum has.

Underneath our two front windows
a puzzle of concrete pieces lay a foundation.
We decided on art, but definitely not high brow
and set off to look at a yard art location.
        At one we found a metal raven, named Regn,
        perched upon stone, then off to look again.

We put in sidewalk chunks, tore bushes apart
to host metal and stone work along the house.
We wanted art which stole our heart.
We will take months no doubt to browse.
        We plunked a butterfly whirligig in stony pot,
        added Snively Snail and Tucker Turtle to the spot.

More like a walkway than familiar patios,
figures can be added to parade.
How many? Who knows?
Helen Hedgehog made the grade.
        I enjoy the cheerful cluster--
        a sure bad mood buster.

We want to line the pathway with pizzaz
but not a very valuable, rob-able display.
Plenty of room for more razz-a-ma-tazz.
Our search is still underway.
        The centerpiece requires a new decision.
        The whole project is open to revision,

like our inside mini-museum has
with thousands of creatures, lots of angels.
We won't clutter the yard as much, whereas
we'll see if yard art's lesser scope gels,
        so drivers and passersby can see
        art of whimsical creativity.

Feline Archaeologist

Neighbor's cat stares at our new yard art.
        Front yard oopart?

Metal and concrete animals--
        odd examples.

Cat pauses and takes paws away.
        Will these things stay?

Cat visited the other day
when there were bushes not creatures
with unanimated features.
Front yard oopart, odd examples–will these things stay?

Hatchimals

A Hatchimal- a furry, walking, talking bird that hatches from a shell.

Santa's searching globally to fill his bag
for the most desired gift to be had.
Parent helpers scour Internet, to snag
Hatchimals –they are the latest fad.
       In this digital, plastic time,
       hand-held Hatchimals are prime.

For the most desired gift to be had
Facebook's Hatchimal Support Groups
and Hatchimal Addicts report sightings, glad
to have someone to commiserate with, troops
       who sell and trade these birds
       nurturing hatching herds and nerds.

Parent helpers scour Internet to snag
any Hatchimal from its nest to un-shell.
No time to defer price gouging, lollygag.
Hatchimals even have a Youtube channel.
       Toy hunters increase employment
       to provide a child's brief enjoyment.

Hatchimals, they are the latest fad–
Cabbage Patch dolls, Barbie and Ken,
Disney creatures, action figures clad
in magical powers, Tickle-me Elmo–then
       toys were still a momentary craze
       enjoyed during a growing-up phase.

In this digital, plastic time
of miniature-sized gadgets, mechanical toys,
Pokeman-Go, while screen contacts climb–
Hatchimals are one of mechandisers' ploys,
       to channel children's imagination--
       not create-your-own-toy determination.

Hand-held Hatchimals are prime,
but kids hold real animals' fates in their hands--
they could adopt or sponsor an animal sometime,
rather than computer, canned commands.
       Hatchimal Hunters hold their trophies
       as post-holiday interest atrophies.

Gunk Love

Love yourself: shadows and gunk and all. This is how you open your heart. Sara Wiseman

It's hard to love with all our gunk,
bring light to our shadows.
I shmooze with my beloved junk
to find a path love follows.
>   I accept my imperfection.
>   I do not seek for perfection.

Bring light to our shadows
so we don't wallow in the dark.
Find the joy each life allows;
when penned leave for a park.
>   Open your heart wide
>   and you will find love inside.

I schmooze with my beloved junk--
thousands in my miniature museum.
But they're inanimate – most have thunk,
but their up-vibes-- my joyous heirloom.
>   Their color, texture lift like wings.
>   Such happiness each essence brings.

To find a path love follows,
we can expand our circumference,
discover what entities love endows
and change our range of reference.
>   Love inside and outside ourselves
>   depends upon how deep one delves.

I accept my imperfection.
Not all my loved ones and dreams manifest.
Some quests are beyond my detection.
I settle for doing my best.
>   Life can get messy- really yucky.
>   Most the time I think I'm lucky.

I do not seek for perfection--
to do so narrows focus on myself too much.
If love and service are my selection
I need more outreach, more beings to touch.
>   I'll love all kinds of things and creatures
>   to seek out their lovable features.

Requiem for a High School Romance

We were high school sweethearts in the 1950's,
from opposite ends of a suburban Connecticut town.
We were both of Swedish descent, blue-eyed blondes.
We looked like siblings. Tall and short Vikings.

We had two sets of matching plaid shirts.
Both of us went to a church youth group
and sang in the choir. He played the violin.
He drove me to school in a blue convertible.

We went to dances and proms, movies and parties,
endured sharing limited time on family phones,
and could only date on weekends. We had chosen
our pen names for when we became writers.

He made me a wooden box for love notes and valentines.
We had a photo album of our courtship.
We drew plans for our Connecticut home.
I created our family in red yarn with braided limbs--
octopuses with yellow hair, our four children
with a marble inside their heads.
        I kept all the mementoes
        when we broke up in 1958
        shortly after the Senior Prom.

I wanted to go to college to become a teacher.
I did not believe in sex before marriage
and I was too young to marry.
I was not willing to waiver from my goal.

Our mothers attended the Swedish-American club.
For decades I learned tidbits about him.
        When he looked at me at graduation, he cried.
        One of his lungs collapsed from smoking when young.
        He married a college classmate and had two children.
        He built his home in Connecticut, while I had moved West.

Shortly afterwards he came to visit me
at my summer job, but I was not receptive.
One week after our breakup, I went on my only
blind double date with friends and met the man
I would marry three years later after college.
He was one year ahead of me at the same high school.
I had read his palm at a Y fundraiser, we realized. Fate?

After a year I received a letter from my ex
requesting a dinner date, but by then
I was dating my future husband,
who my mother favored. She told me
not to go and helped me craft a response.
She was afraid he would win me back.
I should have gone to have closure.

My grandmother said I should not marry a Swede.
We should spice up our bland blood– marry an Italian.
Well, my husband is English, Irish, German descent
and our children are pale Europeans.

After several decades my mother revealed
my ex-boyfriend had come to the house
several times wanting to see me.
Once I was in the backyard. She sent him away.
One time he came with a kitten,
my mother refused to give me.
I did not know this and felt badly.
I should have talked with him.

In the almost sixty years since I last saw him,
many times I wanted to send him a note of apology
and send copies of photos from the album
for his children to see him when he was young.
I thought maybe at a high school reunion
he would be there. He never came when I was there.
When I went East to visit family and friends,
I thought perhaps I should call, but never did.

In the fall of 2016 I went East again.
A friend told me he had died in the spring.
She said his obituary mentioned community work.
I always believed he would become a good man,
but I had made a better choice for me–
a truly wonderful man of integrity and kindness.

Now it is too late to tell him I'm sorry
for hurting him and to thank him
for a loving, chivalrous, mostly happy,
old-fashioned, youthful romance.

When I returned home, I could not find
his obituary on the Internet. Dead or alive
I decided to let unresolved memories fade.

Mother's Day

My brothers and I
bought our mother, Honey
a potted pansy each year.

Even when grown and a continent
apart, her children would call and card.
Siblings in the same state would bring
a bouquet for her dining room table.

This year not only is my mother
gone for several years,
but both brothers died last May.

One brother's wife will be
able to celebrate Mother's Day.
My brothers and I will never again
plant pansies, bring bouquets for Honey.

This year will be especially
sad for me as I wait to go to lunch
with my children and grandchildren,
missing my mother and brothers.

These Are My Wishes For You
From a letter from Helen Erickson Varsell

Found in a file of poem fragments
was a photo copy of a hand-written letter
from my mother. I wonder where the original is?
I wonder if these are her words or
she found this essay and copied it for me.
I decided to line it like a love poem.
Somehow I was to re-discover this now.

May you find serenity and tranquility
in a world you may not always understand.
May the pain you have known and the conflict
you have experienced give you the strength
to walk through life facing each new situation
with courage and optimism.
Always know that there are those whose love
and understanding will always be there
even when you feel most alone.

May you discover enough goodness in others
to believe in a world of peace.
May a kind word, a reassuring touch
and a warm smile be yours every day
of your life, and may you give these gifts
as well as receive them.

Remember the sunshine when the storm
seems unending.
Teach love to those who know hate,
and let love embrace you
as you go into the world.

May the teachings of those you admire
become part of you so that you can call on them.
Remember those whose lives you have touched
and those who have touched you
are always a part of you, even if the encounters
were less than you would have wished.
It is in the content of the encounter
that is more important than the form.

May you not be too concerned about material matters,
but instead place immeasurable value
on the goodness of your heart.
Find time each day to see beauty and love
in the world around you.
Realize that each person has limitless abilities,
but that each one of us is different
in our own way.

Whatever you feel you may lack in the present
may become one of your strengths in the future.
May you see your future fill
with promise and possibility.
Learn to review everything in a worthwhile experience.
May you find enough inner strength
to determine your own worth by yourself
and not depend on another's judgment
of your accomplishments.
May you always feel loved.

Perhaps these are someone else's words
my mother felt would be meaningful for me.
She embedded them in me.
The letter is undated, uncredited and unsigned
but it is in my mother's cursive.
She even crossed out and corrected in two spots.
Having re-found this at age 77 decades after her death,
I see these words are an outline of my quest
for meaning and understanding
and I am living much of which she has loved to me.

Moonstruck

Is it the gift of the gods straight from paradise? The ancient Aztecs were convinced.
So you see it's only natural to crave Moonstruck Dark Chocolate. To resist is futile.
Moonstruck Dark Chocolate wrapper

Amen. Thank you gods.
I must have been an Aztec
in a former life. I'm just
doing what comes naturally–
another moonstruck lover.

I can rationalize in so many ways
why I should or should not be
a dark chocolate worshipper.
I am not trying to convince
anyone of its merits or demerits.

I do prefer dark chocolate
supposedly more healthy
but I do not care.
I like the taste, energy
and up-mood components.

I can look at the sky
with dark Milky Ways: perhaps space junk
stars: dark M and M's, moon pie,
travel the cosmos for more chocolate flavors,
but I am happy with dark chocolate close by.

Midnight Mischief

After a high-temperature day
my husband opened the windows
to let night air cool the room
      where my collection of angels
      dangle from the ceiling
      sprawl on walls and surfaces.

Thunder added lightning to set
the stage. Gusts of wind
blew paper angels to the floor,
      dripped sticky dots with numbers to register
      then when they joined the angelic troop–
      specks splattered the floor like snowflakes.

Wind wrestled with wind chimes
melodically clanking a rhythm
for angel dancing, awakening me
      to rouse to the scene, hope for calm.
      It was clear the air-freed angels
      would not stop falling until all was still.

I grumbly stared at the tumbled angels.
White dots speckled blue carpet.
Numbered dots could not be re-attached.
      Specks needed to be swept. Chimes ceased.
      Slowly wind-dusted angels resumed their positions.
      No need to dust. I closed the windows–smiling.

Shifting Light

Holly leaves sparkle in sunlight,
cinquant as a lighted Christmas tree.
Later in the afternoon, the sun shifts
and dazzles golden sparks
on the other side's sun-reaching branches.

The window frames this glistening display,
catches light and shadow dancing.
On the sill two unlit electric candles
await the switch turning on at night
with moonlit darkened leaves and berries.

Addressing Book Access

Soon-summer reminds me
to re-install my poetry cache box
with free poems for passers-by.

They can sit on the sidewalk chunk wall
to read while resting from their walk or
take poems with them at their leisure.

All over our town tiny mini-libraries
like bird houses let book-lovers
take donated books from their yard perches.

People who live inside have shelves
of books collected and protected from weather,
cherished when reading in comfortable places.

People who have an address
or go to school have access
to book loans in libraries.

People who live outside, homeless
rely on Street Books bringing books
by bicycle in a wooden wagon.

These readers can be in public libraries
during certain hours, but can't take books
with them for they have no address for a card.

Not everyone has a computer for e-books.
There are many types of addresses
some people do not have.

I need to increase the circulation
for some of my books to book sales,
gifts to friends, donations to libraries–all sizes.

People living inside and outside
can share books I own and write.
I need to address book access.

I will start with the poetry cache,
increase my donations, design a mini-library
to stand side-by-side under cover.

The Unreadable Book

The Voynich Manuscript believed written in the 15th century by Jacob Tepenecz ,
a chemist. No one, even professional cryptographers can decipher the text.

On my bookshelves are many unread books.
I could read my books, if I put them in my to-read pile.
The Voynich Manuscript, even if it looks
great on-line, I'd never comprehend his style.
When he wrote a book no one can read
is it a hoax, secret or just mystery indeed?

I could read my books, if I put them in my to-read pile.
Some have been on the shelf for years.
Others are favored, so it might take a while
before my gaze upon them appears.
But Jacob wrote and illustrated a manuscript
in language and images seemingly nondescript.

The Voynich Manuscript, even if it looks
like it might contain some important message,
so far we do not know from any outlooks
the code, invented letters, formula or adage.
Strange plants, small naked women bathing,
astrological aspects, with no mistakes, reveal nothing.

Great on-line, I'd never comprehend his style
though it is available for ponderous viewing,
pages clearly at the website--meanwhile,
leaving all the scholars and voyeurs stewing.
Alchemist secret, traveler's shorthand, universal language?
Called MS 408 at Yale, Voynicheros explore every passage.

When he wrote a book no one can read,
did he hide cliff notes or code someone could crack?
Many other authors suspected, none succeed,
claim it is a forgery, but consensus appears to back
it is genuine from inks, paper and binding
and all the high-tech clues they are finding.

Is it a hoax, secret or just mystery indeed?
The 40 or so characters remain unknown.
Was Jacob just a playful, erudite breed,
keeping all his discoveries his own?
Most writers hope to be read
but remain in obscurity instead.

I Like What Mr. Rogers Says

When I say its you I like, I'm talking about that part of you that knows that life is far more than anything you can ever see or hear or touch. That deep part of you that allows you to stand for those things without which humankind cannot survive. Love that conquers hate, peace that rises triumphant over war, and justice proves more powerful than greed.   Fred Rogers

Mr. Rogers valued the beautiful, noble and sacred.
Deep and simple is better than shallow and complex.
Look for the helpers when you are scared.
I like you just the way you are, Rogers reflects.
>Children need time to create and play,
>to discover who they are in a reflective way.

Deep and simple is better than shallow and complex
in a surface society of pollution and screens.
Media turning us into consumers, people perplex.
What is behind those flat, noisy scenes?
>Mister Rogers created a tranquil neighborhood,
>to sort things out the best he could.

Look for the helpers when you are scared.
Even the newscasts share some positive segments,
about people who stepped up and prepared
to help and heal when an event fragments.
>We can choose to align with bearers of light,
>connect with those who uplift and invite.

I like you just the way you are, Rogers reflects
as he opens doors to himself and for others.
He welcomes, affirms as he introspects,
asks us to support one another.
>His puppet world feels real.
>His approaches for children -- ideal.

Children need time to create and play–
not constant digital distraction.
Time to see problems solved in a kind way.
Time to witness positive interaction.
>Mr. Rogers is timeless, warm as his sweater.
>I value the time we spent together.

To discover who they are in a reflective way,
children need quiet time to create and think,
ponder the values that become their mainstay
when powerful waves push them to the brink.
>"What is essential is invisible to the eye".
>Mr. Rogers was a deep-seeing guy.

Cloudy Weather

Climate Changes

The ground we walk on,
the plants and creatures,
the clouds above
constantly dissolving
into new formations—
each a gift of nature
possessing its own
radiant energy,
bound together
by cosmic harmony.

Ruth Barnard

Reverence

If we perceived Life with reverence, we would stand in awe at the experience of physical Life and walk the Earth in a very deep sense of gratitude. Gary Zukav

Reverence expresses our higher intention
to treat Life with gratitude and respect.
Do Earthlings need an intervention,
to become less violent, more introspect?
>> Beyond spirituality to the essence of being,
>> reverence requires a new way of seeing.

To treat Life with gratitude and respect
like many of our ancestors did,
who found ways to sustain and connect,
perceive the cosmos as splendid,
>> could make modern living more grateful,
>> less suffering, less wasteful, less hateful.

Do Earthlings need an intervention?
Gaia stresses with climate change,
mining, pollution, lack of prevention.
Physical life needs to rearrange
>> priorities, actions, future goals,
>> seek solutions and place some controls.

To become less violent, more introspect
might encourage more reverence.
Gratitude is hard to expect
when one sees no deliverance,
>> from darkness, toxic atmosphere.
>> Many live in pain and fear.

Beyond spirituality to the essence of being,
some experience reverence and gratitude.
While patiently applying solutions, freeing,
some do find an appreciative attitude.
>> Some conditions are truly appalling,
>> require assistance, a higher calling.

Reverence requires a new way of seeing
beneath the surfaces' challenges with hope.
Dig within to express, set despair fleeing.
Reverence could be a good way to cope.
>> To view reality with awe, as a miracle--
>> could create a revolution, avoid a debacle.

Playing Keep Away

Why
angels
fly
away
from humans
could be
we
pollute
their air space,
make them cough, choke,
bonk with drones,
plunk space
junk.
Dodging
keeps them aloft,
on ground
we'd
knock them
out.

The Unseen and Unborn

Make my poems for others unseen and unborn. Muriel Rukeyser

Last night was a rare Supermoon,
but it was shrouded in clouds.
Fortunately I had seen it the night before
as it shone, luminously unblemished.
Today I saw a double-rainbow
en route to a regular check-up.

I planned to write about the Supermoon.
But due to the election, my mind also clouds.
Never saw a worse campaign before.
No one remains unblemished.
Can I see any hope in a double-rainbow?
The whole nation needs a thorough check-up.

Many people did not see the Supermoon.
The whole world's vision clouds.
We have seen disastrous politics before.
No nation's record is unblemished.
Yet everyone wants promise of a double-rainbow.
Gaia needs a global and cosmic check-up.

Will the unseen and unborn witness a Supermoon?
Will our unknowing remain in the clouds?
Will the planet and people ever be unblemished?
Will we continue to act as we have before?
Will climate change and pollution taint any rainbow?
Our souls need better diagnoses, a cleansing check-up.

Supermoon
November 2016

Clouds shroud supermoon--.
next in thirty-four
years.

I doubt I will be alive.
Let moonlight festoon!
Took sneak peak

near its peak.
Again seek
light–unique.
Bright glow gone too soon.

Cloudy

A cloud learns not to look down. Andrea Cohen

Clouds are sky-sponges
     soak up pollution   slurp seas
         absorb toxic ingredients.

Smothered in smoke and smog   a blurry slurry
     pierced by rocket bullets   satellite scratches
         endure space junk plummeting through.

Atmosphere penetrates cloud-tops where angels traipse
     turmoil roils   disturbs their resting spot
         between delivering messages.

Cloud-bottoms drop acid rain   Strain rain
     heave hail   splay snow and sleet
         descend mist and fog.

Clouds clutch,   bunch   blanche and gray
    thin   Swashes of sunrise and sunset
         array auroras   conjure ghostly images.

Eyelids for stars   Shadow sun rays
     contrails streak linear imitations
         Clouds endure turbulence   whirlwinds

Clouds attack.   throughways for meteorites   stir storms
     hurl hurricanes   flash floods   clash cyclones
         twirl tornados   witness damage below

Recycling receiver and rejecter   Clouds manipulate moods.
     When clouds look down   a rainbow frown
         Clouds look up to cosmos for rescue.

Sensational Clouds

You can read about all the purposes of clouds
their effect on weather, water cycle, protection.
But I like clouds to stir curiosity,
create mood and deep reflection.

I don't like contrails scarring sky,
or pollution smudging their beauty.
I like cleansing rain, clear blue atmosphere
with gauzy clouds on duty.

I like to imagine creatures
in these billowing, dynamic cloudscapes.
Abstract art, technicolor expressions,
dazzling divine followed escapes.

Anytime of day or night
whenever light reveals their design,
clouds can uplift my thoughts
and with my best intentions align.

Clouds play peekaboo with sun and moon,
they display sensational light.
Whenever they are seeable
they bring intense delight.

Bruised Sky

After a day of cloud bunching and punching
        the bruised sky
                sunsets into night

This afternoon four contrails
two diffusing, two crisp
from racing parallel planes
scar the sky
        quotation marks on blue

Pollution exhausts atmosphere
        bleeds acid rain
                gasps breath

Mystery in the Clouds
Cloud of the Month: November 2016

What is that peculiar, gaped-toothed jaw in the clouds?
It appears like a curve, a u-shape–
a partial ring. An aerial crop circle?

The formation's like foggy cars on a carnival ride,
part of a necklace, castle turrets, crown, curved vertebrae–
regular lumps or lobes with no other half?

The lobes hung from the underside of a cloud layer
at Hampton Lucy over Warwickshire, England.
The Cloud Appreciation Society made it Cloud of the Month.

Gavin Pretor-Pinney is a cloud detective
of the Cloud Appreciation Society who sought
to solve the mystery of these strange clouds.

He determined they were not natural–
not "mammas" from the underside
of a storm cloud canopy.

He focused on aircraft. Planes fly through
clouds of super-cooled water droplets which freeze,
leave gaps, a dissipation trail or distrail?

The regular spacing of the lobes might be condensation
trails caused by two swirling vortices produced
by wings, rotating opposite in the aircraft's wake?

Two turbulent flows interact, combine
to form downdraft patterns which appear
as lobes below a condensation trail?

This mystery was caused by aircraft flying
just above the base of cloud layers as it turned
in a holding pattern at a nearby airport.

The plane's condensation trail was hidden
within the cloud layer, cloud-lobes descending
below it, caused by wing turbulence.

Wing-whirled clouds? Planes etch straight contrails.
Inside cloud banks, we fly in gauzy space.
Cloud mysteries create many patterns.

I am mostly a ground cloud observer,
wondering what pollution clouds gather before
raining it back to us in a mysterious cycle.

The Cloud Appreciation Society Manifesto

We believe that clouds are unjustly maligned
and that life would be immeasurable poorer without them.

We think that they are Nature's poetry and the most
egalitarian of her displays since everyone can have
a fantastic view of them.

We pledge to fight "blue-sky" thinking wherever
we find it. Life would be dull if we had to look up
at cloudless monotony day after day.

We remind people that clouds are expressions
of the atmosphere's moods and can be read
like those of a person's countenance.

We believe that clouds are for dreamers
and their contemplation benefits the soul.
Indeed, all who consider the shapes they see in them
will save money on psychoanalysis bills.

Look up, marvel at the ephemeral beauty
and always remember to live life
with your head in the clouds.

My Cloud Appreciation Manifesto

Clouds clean up our messes, churn, rinse, wring dry,
flood, storm, recycle our pollution, remind us
to pay attention and be sustainable.

Clouds are Nature's poetry scrawling sky,
configurations reflecting Gaia's mood
and cosmic handiwork sparking the muses.

Clouds evoke "blue-sky thinking" when
seasons and thoughts gather light, puffed
or layered, some prefer seeing blue than gray.

Clouds create an atmosphere above and below.
We can heed the changes, reflect and act
in the best interest of the planet and its inhabitants.

Clouds are for all-ages dreamers be they artists,
writers, scientists, futurists, ponderers, wonderers.
We all dwell in the cloud of unknowing.

Clouds lure us to look up, take flight, imagine
what is possible. Bubbling, straightened clouds
of infinite diversity, coloring our day, illuminating night.

Bonding with Nature

We cannot win this battle to save species and environments without forging an emotional bond between ourselves and nature as well–for we will not fight to save what we do not love. Jay Gould

Nature is easy to love when
not in a tsunami, tornado,
earthquake, hurricane or
any natural disaster.

But we have polluted the air,
created garbage dumps in the sea,
war-torn the surface, piped, mined,
provoked pesticide, concrete, asphalt attacks.

Nature is feared and loved.
Climate change demands sustainability,
adaptability, new ways of thinking.
Perhaps not viewing nature as a battle?

When nature acts up, it is often renewal.
Our challenge is to be prepared and react
not adding destructive acts into the mix.
Might start with love and respect for all creation.

If we move to an age of connection,
cooperation and compassion, nature
and all earthly relationships can flourish.
Is this a possible reality or an illusion?

The planet can survive without people.
It did so for millions of years and can again.
Will we be good Earth guests
or get off the planet before evicted?

In just the observable universe
there are at least 2 trillion other galaxies.
Perhaps our souls can maneuver another body
or float non-physically through space.

But wondrous, beautiful, life-breathing Earth
is the only home we are aware of now.
When species go extinct, landscapes scraped,
air and sea contaminated –we should care and love.

A Rainy Windy Autumnal Day

Leaves flutter on the branches
like a flock of birds
flickering in the wind.

Leaves fly in formation
until released by tethers
scampering while grounding.

I watch a scrawny stripling
almost bare from the middle upward.
Bottom half clings cover.

Unclad trunk shakes its limbs
of any garish garment
throwing patches to the earth.

Undressing before me
I enjoy the strip-tease.
Drive away gustily.

The Slow Invasion

Snails are not native to the Pacific Northwest.
Many were imported by Europeans specialists attest.
French vineyard introducer of escargot provides details-
became a "Johnny Appleseed of snails".

Northwest gardens confront hungry snails.
Gardeners poison, salt, foot impales.
Invasive species numbers are unknown.
Some land snails and slug cousins aren't native grown.

Homegrown native species live in the forest.
Its non-native pests that infest.
Synthropic snails associate with agriculture.
Gardeners are the snail's vulture.

Scientists dissect them to remove teeth
to see what identification lies beneath.
No matter what snail species they are–
even slugs are victims of voracious war.

Lancetooth snail has raspy teeth, tugs
other snails from shells as well as kills slugs.
Native slugs: banana and self-amputating tail dropper
would applaud any breed of snail stopper.

Pie plates filled with beer
drown snails as gardeners cheer.
Guzzling gastropods gorge at night.
Water morning, reduce plight.

Rake garden early to expose eggs
to elements and in reach of bird's legs.
Salt and chemicals make them fatally sick.
Perhaps edge of trowel or foot kinder and quick.

My husband does husbandry of our organic yard.
I am just the inside job, a slow-moving bard.
I do not much care the snail-paced species' name,
we move sluggishly together– all the same.

Tardigrades, the Indestructible

This microorganism is the size of a period.
Found all over the world where others don't go.
To us funny-looking "water bears", odd.
Scientists should not treat them so.
>   Tardigrades are slow steppers, amblers,
>   eight-legged, rolly-polly scramblers

Found all over the world where others won't go–
airless Himalayas, Antarctic ice, deep sea trenches,
murky pond in New York's Central Park, also
moss, dirt, dust from street and benches.
>   Unbearable conditions for us not them.
>   These water bears have a survival anthem.

To us funny-looking "water bears" odd
because we can dig them, freeze them
yet they revive in a petri dish. When prod
they awake, lay eggs, their own stratagem.
>   Sleeping Beauties awake in warm bath.
>   Scientists stunned at the aftermath.

Scientists should not treat them so.
Freeze, starve, squish, burn–
blast them with radiation glow.
Dry and rehydrate them, also
>   rocket them into space–
>   such treatment a disgrace.

Tardigrades are slow steppers, amblers.
For decades they were frozen in subzero.
But when revived scientists saw scampers.
They are a nature poster hero.
>   Some people find stubby legs, squashed face cute.
>   Perhaps their vision is not very acute.

Eight-legged, roly-poly scramblers
are lauded for their indestructibility.
These world-wide mini-ramblers
are wondrous in their ability
>   to find a place almost anywhere on Earth.
>   Earthlings, give them a welcome berth.

Crazy Snake Worms

Don't Go West, Asian jumping worms
from eastern to western Oregon!
Also called Crazy snake worms,
they now greet rain, left sun.

They are considered an invasive species.
They don't feed deep in the soil
like native earthworms. They dine shallow
on forest floor detritus, cause turmoil.

Forests need this top layer
for forest health, water retention,
it beds nutrients for seed germination
for forest regeneration.

These slim, worm-wigglers wildly thrash,
can levitate off the ground.
Perhaps these nuisance nibblers would be
less annoying if they fed underground.

They reproduce asexually,
so populations will quickly grow.
Ridgy, forest share-croppers,
hard-to-stoppers, where will they go?

Oh, the Chimneys

When Vaux's swifts fly from Canada to Mexico--
100 miles between stops, they need
the insides of old chimneys, they know
to perch vertically, not new chimneys, indeed,
       because night temperature drops
       they must huddle inside at their stops.

100 miles between stops they need
not new lined chimneys, impossible for foothold,
but vanishing old brick chimneys to succeed
to cluster close, conserve heat from the cold.
       But redevelopment, seismic concerns
       their guano and noise–no smoke burns.

The insides of old chimneys they know
disappear from slick urban landscape.
Brick smoke stacks before 1940 -- long ago
were torn down, capped, now no escape.
       Old growth forest destruction also
       provides them fewer places to go.

To perch vertically (not new chimneys, indeed)
leaves diminishing hollowed out trees.
Only 4 inches long, grayish-brown breed
with black eye patch, crescents in air-- agrees
       with bird watchers as swifts sweep and swirl
       into dark chimneys with pulsating twirl.

Because night temperature drops
swifts like ominous black cloud, flow into one chimney.
Thousands crowd into place within chosen props,
still several respites on their migratory journey.
       Fewer birds in recent years.
       Loss of choices fuels fears.

They must huddle inside their stops
like gas chamber victims of the holocaust.
Millions of people passed the nonstops
whose survival options were all lost,
       whose bodies were tossed to ditches from gurneys,
       whose ashes smoked through grim-rimmed chimneys.

The News This Earthweek
Week ending December 16, 2016

Each week I read the Earthweek:
Diary of a Changing World column.
Each week the news is dire,
I react with sadness, remain solemn.

This week many global earthquakes,
as Mt. St. Helen's shook- recharging.
The North Pole's temperature rising
twice as fast. Melting discharging.

More animals facing extinction.
Giraffes rapidly dwindling with habitat
and poaching. Reindeer shrinking,
becoming thin as Santa remains fat.

A supercolony of Ethiopian ants show signs
of formations to invade other parts of world.
Ants could hitchhike on tourist's luggage.
One pregnant queen-- and havoc unfurled.

A lethal Bengal cyclone brought
high winds and torrential rainfall.
Across US an arctic storm dumped
rain, snow and ice on us all.

That is just this week in brief
not dealing with political changes,
economics, other human endeavors,
drilling and pollution exchanges.

I can stop reading and viewing news,
not witness the catastrophic events, clues
to climate and human changes
that bring on the heart-wrenching blues.

Some days I tune out, cocoon,
take a sensory sabbatical,
focus on creativity and art,
avoid actions overly violent and radical.

Myriad realities and multiple dimensions
promise escape, light grid in place.
Maybe we need to heal Earth first,
explore inner and outer space.

Gaia's Keepers

Earthlings are the Keepers of Gaia
the guardians of this Earth.
So get into gear! We're out of here
if we don't clear up our acts and berth?

Earthlings breed billions of people.
How can Earth sustain us all?
We're out of here? So get into gear,
if we don't heed a new protocol.

Earthlings need to be sustainable,
stop polluting air, land, sea.
So get into gear. We're out of here
if we don't act responsibly.

Earthlings face doom, catastrophe
from sky, as well as planet.
We're out of here? So get into gear.
What we can control–just ban it!

Earthlings seek enlightenment, courage
to face our dark challenges.
Get into gear. We're out of here
if we don't change. Gaia revenges.

Yearning for Eden: Earth

Some days when my mindscape appears rocky,
I wonder why I chose the Third Rock from the Sun
for this incarnation. The cosmos is infinite,
surely I had other choices,
other places I could grow.

I entered a world of duality,
confusion and illusion,
planted shiny roots
from being transported
so often from other gardens.

But this time when I chose
form, time and place
I must have hoped Eden was real
when I viewed beautiful Earth's
prospectus to lure inhabitants.

When I found out people
were not stewards but destroyers
and Earth's air, water, land
are polluted, I wish I had
chosen to be a rock.

Cloudbursts

Global Gleanings

The myth of unlimited production
brings war in its train
as inevitably
as clouds announce a storm.

Albert Camus

Uncontrollable?

Surrounded in my light cocoon
I take a rest this afternoon,
protected, illuminated from the dark
I try to ignite a creative spark.

Radiating from my cradled core
I cut loose–explore
                    UNCONTROLLABLE.
Each mini-bit of energy
          seeks connection or free-flow.

Will my thoughts fall into form?
          Free-ranging?   Jostle?   Connect?
Release my energy, full blast–
          I want to: dangle, dandle,
                    wrangle, entangle.

I can't control my consciousness
          super or sub consciousnesses.
Matter manifests- often uncontrollable.
          My tech-turd tools unmanageable.

I spend so much time
          trying to gain control
of my actions, compose free verse or rhyme
          while I seek a new protocol.

Winging-it,   playfully toss things around
          Listen to sound.   Images abound.

I'm not a consistent regulator
          rather a whimsical participator
            persistent mood elevator
          gather light escalator
            resistant darkness excavator

An uncontrollable experimenter
    poetry form discoverer   word-play inventor
enthusiast of art, skating and gymnastics, dance
    not totally comfortable leaving things to chance.

Curiosity,   creativity guide my way
    not likely to herd, follow others.
I like to lead, teach, positively sway–
    not deal with negativity, if have my druthers.

If with a paddle board
    I like to be bouncing ball on a string
not gripping hand tight
    I want to spring.

            I want to be open
            not over-filter
            find some calm
            when world's off-kilter.

Why must everything be under control?
Judged. Competitive. Stick to rigid rules?
Release serendipity, coincidence cosmically ensouled.
    Fly in atmosphere.   Breathe in pools.

Just what is the essence of our reality?
How much can we be in charge?
How much is beyond our comprehending?
    Perhaps the percentage is extremely large.

I delight in speculating otherworldly realms,
other dimensions, under cosmic entities' helms.
We have very little understanding of the unknown.
    Some people still believe we are alone.

My soul could be eternally free,
not controlled much by this sliver of me.
        That is if I am a soul-splinter
        and I have a guardian hinter.

So I'm left to conclude I can't
        be a control freak.
Some oozing of spirit
        is bound to leak.

So I ponder what to control if I could,
what I want to, can or even should.
Neither totally controllable or limited free
if I follow a personal or cosmic plan. I would?

So for now I relish
        what makes me happy,
try to avoid the hellish
        to pursue luminosity.

Controllable?   Uncontrollable?

Night-Shine

Noctilucent clouds glow early this year.
Night-shining clouds, electric blue
seen in southern atmosphere.
Climate change illuminates through.

Night-shining clouds, electric blue
were not recorded before 1885.
Now spacecraft over Antarctica found clue.
Shocking blue sunlit clouds arrive.

Now seen in southern atmosphere
previously seen in Seattle, Estonia, Glascow,
ice crystals and dust in the mesosphere
viewed after sunset, before sunset somehow.

Climates change illuminates through,
because greenhouse gases warm lower levels.
Upper levels are cool. Clouds bright hue's due
to pollution. What head-in-the-clouds foretells?

Mushrooming Clouds

During the nuclear testing era, troops were exposed to detonations to see how they would react to a nuclear attack and whether equipment would still function....Scientists had known from the earliest testing that radiation posed risks..increased rates of cancer among survivors of the Japanese bombings. Jennifer LeFleur

Nuclear tests and bombs mushroom clouds
over atolls, islands, deserts, Japan.
This is not a legacy of which to be proud.
Service members become "atomic veterans".
   Civilians and military die, become ill.
   We are dealing with the casualties still.

Over atolls, islands, desert, Japan–
over 200 above-ground, underwater tests.
400,000 military took part in the plan.
Pilots flew through, some cleaned up, frogmen attest.
   Recklessly exposed to nuclear radiation
   atomic veterans need care from this nation.

This is not a legacy of which to be proud
to have inflicted on anyone.
Radiation has created a shroud
on the next generation.
   Vets' children and grandchildren suffer effects.
   Some health claims the government rejects.

Service members become atomic veterans
some of them and their families receive no compensation.
We are generating radiated clans--
over-shadowed victims with no participation.
   Only 21 types of cancers qualify
   Others illnesses? They don't apply.

Civilians and military die, become ill.
We contaminated planet and atmosphere.
Troops exposed to detonations, fulfill
tasks not knowing risks and full dangers there.
   Atomic vets were sworn to secrecy for decades,
   with little recognition for sacrifices, no accolades.

We are dealing with the casualties still.
We still have wars, tests, vets, damaged DNA.
Does our nation have the collective will
to use nuclear power in a less devastating way?
   No more radiating mushrooms, charred animals, "guinea pigs", blast sites,
   glassed sand, shock waves, fire burning clouds, flash too bright.

184

Shaping Up Clouds

Clouds contain many possible configurations,
They have Latinate, tongue-twister names.
I think of the shapes for their designations.
Five physical forms comprise their claims.
        Clouds not only in our solar system.
        Exo-planets may have cloud mayhem.

They have Latinate, tongue-twister names
like thin opaque Translucidus. thick opacus
and thick opague Perlucidus-- opacity-based aims.
Clouds in rows converge at horizon for Radiatus
        Patterns of Intorus. Vertebratus
        in combinations or Duplicatus.

I think of the shapes for their designations-
billows, wisps, waves, layers, ripples, rolls, patches,
heaps, tufts, ragged, vortex sheets in endless transformations.
I don't remember what scientific name matches.
        Liquid droplets, frozen crystals fall.
        All their manifestations I can't recall.

Five physical forms comprise their claims.
They morph and combine – harder to pronounce.
Vigas before precipitation reaches ground proclaims
it's Praecipitatis when it hits ground to pounce.
        Mamma feature has bubbly, bulging bottom
        Tuba are funnel column from bottom --- Humm.

Clouds not only in our solar system.
Clouds here can be surfed in glider aircraft.
If on other planets, new research could stem
from surfed data from our spacecraft.
        Clouds of ammonia, sulfur and methane.
        What other surprises will we gain?

Exo-planets may have clouds mayhem.
We add biomass burning, large fires, city lights, auroras, pollution.
Cloud coloration and incident light usually the same.
Aerosol loading changes droplet size and distribution.
        Clouds are part of water cycle, protect atmosphere.
        We better shape up and try to help clouds clear.

Cloud-Catchers

What lurks around clouds?
Sky-scrubbers of pollution,
veils for contrails, cosmic shrouds
for peek-a-boos with moon and sun,
        lair of angels, fairy loft.
        space junk landing soft?

Sky-scrubbers of pollution,
where does cloud toss sieved debris?
The dirtied particles gauzed. Any solution
to the particulates carried in the breeze?
        Meteors, comets satellites' entry discards
        burn, gouge and plunk sea and yards.

Veils for contrails, cosmic shrouds
from rockets, smudges for weather changes,
clouds find our aircraft overcrowds
the sky. Sky-scape rearranges.
        Planes and drones whirl and whip
        the clouds. Perhaps alien starship?

For peek-a-boos with moon and sun
clouds are eyelids, places to go undercover.
Clouds stretch and bunch, color creation.
Clouds could provide a portal cover.
        Who knows what entities conceal,
        disperse or manifest to reveal?

Lair of angels, fairy loft,
winged-beings on a puffy-fluffy vacation,
place to repair, renew in cloudy croft
before return to light-filled vocation.
        Magical beings emanate from clouded minds.
        People delight in these ethereal kinds.

Space junk landing soft
as if cloud cushion provided a brake.
Metallic detritus does not remain aloft,
scars clouds along with contrails. Earthlings awake!
        As you hover unsustainably below,
        don't forsake our cloud pillow.

15 September 11th's
    Oregon, 2016

It was a Sesame Street sunny day
clouds swept away, we were on our way
to visit happy friends where the air is sweet --
a magic carpet ride to where it is beautiful.

It was on such a clear blue sky day
in New York City when the twin towers
crumbled to the ground, a monstrous dust cloud
of toxic ash covered people and debris.

As we drove to our friendly neighbors
where everything's A-OK to play,
flags lined bridges, streets, homes
in remembrance of the horrific event.

At the serene home, we relaxed by a pool,
talking and watching my husband swim.
Rocks rim the pool making it look like a pond.
Sun glistens and the sky is clear.

Many doors opened world wide that day
not just in Sesame Street theme song.
We inhabit an increasingly threatened planet
where beautiful moments are treasured.

When we returned home I watched a documentary
about finding the missing 9/11 flag,
a symbol of the nation's hope and sacrifices-
the courage and bravery of responders and survivors.

I saw the towers fall, Pentagon attack,
plane traffic halted, passengers rushing cockpit
to save the White House and Congress,
all the drama, terror, victims and helpers.

Memorials all over the world, with bits of steel
from Ground Zero, ceremonies at the site.
Blue towers of light, names read, beautiful
buildings–people struggle to be happy, friendly.

We are in the midst of a conflicted presidential election.
Trump said with the twin towers gone, his building
is the tallest in New York City again in 2001. So much changed
in fifteen years. This cannot be 2001's 9/11's legacy.

Turning Off the News

It's hard to turn on television news,
to see in full color blood and blasts.
Newspapers quietly unfold their views,
flatly often with black and white contrasts.
        I can turn the page–move on.
        I can contemplate pro and con.

To see in full color blood and blasts,
terror of violence in people, space, nature–
I witness the impact knowing chaos lasts.
Intolerance erupts from every culture.
        I blanche from these technicolor scenes.
        I want to avoid news from digital screens.

Newspapers quietly unfold their views.
I can choose what I want to read.
Headlines give me hints and clues.
I can follow where my interests lead.
        I hold choices in my vulnerable hands,
        don't push buttons from media demands.

Flatly, often with black and white contrasts
I glaze over photos and shades of gray.
I can skip over negative forecasts,
not let pundits' propaganda sway.
        The state of the world appears dark.
        I look for where light left its mark.

I can turn the page–move on
when my heart pounds and aches.
But if seen on TV or other lexicon
I can't escape the vivid heartbreaks.
        I overload on compassion, diminish by fear,
        anticipate the next explosion to appear.

I can contemplate pro and con
away from TV news coverage.
Just so much stress I can take on.
Where can I apply any leverage?
        Select what to face to my best ability,
        then become informed, take responsibility.

In This Time

The best way to deal with something that is shifting and changing under your feet—whether
it's love, life or art—is just keep dancing   Ann Hornaday

In this time of post-fact, fake news,
hacking, fact check, high tech blues
rather than wake up, some snooze.

In this time when frustrated and confused,
when political correctness is refused,
some trust surrender, some to feeling used.

In this time of world-web connections,
some prefer to make isolated selections,
others seek actions to provide protections.

In this time of chaos and violence,
some act out, some withdraw in silence.
We need better options and resilience.

In this time of climate change,
extinction's and pollution's widening range--
some see others' diversity as strange.

In this time of cosmic discovery,
Earth waits for sustainable recovery.
and for justice, peace, truth's un-covery

In this time we need love and art
to share the planet with open heart,
to dance together not apart.

What is Politically Correct?

Who says just what must be P.C.?
Didn't ask me.

Some fad ideas go viral.
Material

sources not readily assured.
Might be censored.

Whose veracity secured?
Even when explored carefully.
I still might wince and not agree.
Didn't ask me. Material might be censored.

Crumbling

The opposite of love is not hate, it's indifference.   Elie Weisel

Institutions and infrastructure are crumbling.
Old foundations are in decay.
The populace is watching and grumbling.
People seek to build a better way.
>We regress from inaction,
>when we express indifferent reaction.

Old foundations are in decay.
Religions, empires, outdated beliefs
find followers harder to sway.
People swallow or blast their griefs.
>Who will provide insight
>to bring dark issues to light?

The populace is watching and grumbling
at potholes, blackouts, falling bridges.
Agencies lack money, increase fumbling.
Customers face traffic delays, warming fridges.
>Old ideas contain less relevance.
>Some thoughts sustain self-indulgence.

People seek to build a better way,
with cooperation, creativity, compassion.
For Gaia's well-being learn sustainability pays.
Get connection back in fashion.
>With climate change-- act with haste,
>enhance viability, decrease waste.

We regress from inaction,
intolerance, violence and hate.
Solid bases reduce to a fraction.
Some changes we can't accommodate.
>Globalization, population explodes.
>Resources decline, confidence erodes.

When we express indifferent reaction
is it because we are overwhelmed, unaware?
Too full of love or hate for positive action?
Are we overloaded with commitments to care?
>We speculate about our spiraling billions,
>turning into uncontrollable tourbillions.

I Raise Up My Voice

I raise up my voice—not so I can shout but so that those without a voice can be heard...we cannot succeed when half of us are held back. Malala Yousafzai

As the Old World Order crumbles,
a New World emerges,
amid the fears and grumbles,
perhaps the past submerges.
       One day the light shines through--
       the cracks reveal what to do?

A New World emerges
based on justice and diversity,
cooperation. Connection merges
to promote sustainability.
       If hope conquers fear
       the path could clear.

Amid the fears and grumbles
women and children suffer.
As systems and war tumbles,
women remain without a buffer
       against discrimination and violence.
       Their protests met with silence.

Perhaps the past submerges
in some philosophies.
Women promised safety from purges,
but held in check by some theosophies.
       The future could be lighter or darker.
       Abundant or starker. Needs a sparker.

One day the light shines through?
Light-bringers dazzle the world?
Will women get their due?
Will harmony be unfurled?
       Pundits debate whether we can do it
       and if people will live through it.

The cracks reveal what to do?
Let us see the light and take action?
Do we face a hullabulloo or rendezvous,
perhaps a cosmic reaction?
       We must clarify our intention,
       not rely on alien or divine intervention?

Getting Uncontrollable

I'm tired of hierarchy,
        inequity.

Release Old World worn ideas
        rigged medias.

Open thought. Loosen Internet.
        End all regret.

Power structures cast a web-net.
Empower individual.
Create hope, peace, freedom for all.
Inequity, rigged medias–end all regret.

Immigration

By the end of last year, 65 million people displaced.
Root causes are not addressed.
Until conflicts, climate change, economics problems replaced,
the will of the people will be repressed.
>More than half leave from Syria, Somalia, Afghanistan.
>Places for refugees don't have a plan.

Root causes are not addressed.
Too many people, fewer resources re-directed.
Desire for peace, better life expressed.
Political polarization, greed, intolerance suspected.
>Climate change, pollution, waste—
>also part of migrations' haste.

Until conflicts, climate change, economic problems replaced
with cooperative connections, more sustainability,
these issues cannot be erased.
Is the scope beyond our capability?
>Billions of people wondering where to go.
>Will we stage Earth's finale show?

The will of the people will be repressed
as long as fear and divisions prevent unity.
We need global leadership to be pressed
to build a harmonic, prosperous global community.
>Immigration gets blamed for negative hogwash.
>Not an excuse for groups to greenwash.

More than half leave from Syria, Somalia, Afghanistan
unstable places, battlefields of extremist wars.
Violence targeted by surveillance scans.
Water shortages, droughts, eroding shores—
>constant assaults on agriculture,
>conservation make for a shaky future.

Places for refugees don't have a plan.
Globalization not prepared for massive onslaughts.
But are we able to do what we can
to bridge between haves and have nots?
>While pundits ponder theories,
>people left with various miseries.

194

Xenophobia
  2016 Word of the Year   Dictionary.com

To be word of the year it must be a trend,
to have an impact on cultures globally.
Fear of "others", not seeing another as friend--
xenophobia causes many to act very ignobly.
      "I don't like you if you don't look like me"
      does not bring a sense of unity.

To have an impact on cultures globally
xenophobia exhibits hate and disrespect,
fear of difference leads to acts less nobly.
Conflicts over resources makes "others" suspect.
      Various groups become the scapegoat,
      feel unease, revulsion, grabbed by throat.

Fear of "others", not seeing another as friend
leads to harassment, loss the human rights.
Some organizations promote hate, their powers extend
over minorities, discrimination does not end.
      America is not the ideal melting pot.
      There are many groups justice forgot.

Xenophobia causes many to act very ignobly.
White Nationalism, alt right advocate hate,
sexism, racism, intolerance -- most people probably.
Perceived differences lead to protest, debate.
      Rise in xenophobia in part due to globalism,
      climate change, wars, immigration, tribalism.

"I don't like you if you don't look like me."
We're all unique. But hate crimes and Brexit
use immigration, other's beliefs. Don't enjoy diversity.
Economic pressures, violence prompt an exit.
      Americans conquered indigenous people, brought slavery,
      still oppress certain groups in their greed-driven knavery.

Does not bring a sense of unity.
when cyber-bullying and political unrest
shake the foundations of community,
lead to peaceful and destructive protest.
      Xenophobia is a concept to be fought
      or human experiment might be for naught.

Culling Populations

We are culling populations worldwide,
We kill some groups and set others aside.

The government slaughters thousands
of double-breasted cormorants,
shoots them and pours oil on their eggs,
because they eat emblematic salmon
and steelhead, considered endangered.
Their predators like Caspian tern birds
have been relocated. Seal lions
have been caught and euthanized.
Some fishers have restricted access
and quotas. Pyrotechnics at dam
did not work against predators of the salmon
who struggled through Bonneville Dam.

Bats die of nose fungus by millions.
Elephant and rhino tusks go to Asians.
Lion heads poached for trophies.
Wild animals hunted beyond subsistence.
Sea creatures die of inhaling plastic bits,
caught in nets and by over-fishers' discards,
entangle in gyres of garbage.
Birds collide with drones, wind tower power propellers
become targets of sport shooting.
Species go extinct at an alarming rate.

Humans displaced by war and climate change
swarm over land and sea seeking asylum,
survival, protection from violence.
Humans kill each other as well as other species.
People, over-populate into billions,
then endanger whole populations by conflict,
waste, pollution, fighting for rigidly-held views.

People are on the endangered species list.
A politician wants to cull certain groups
from immigrating– those here illegally,
send them back to countries of origin
then build a wall to keep them out.
Dams do not work for salmon.
Walls do not work for people.

We cull populations selectively and randomly decide.
Who will we protect, kill, set aside?

Mass Shootings

About bullies
calculating, destroying
existence frantically.
Guns hitting individuals,
just killing lives,
making normal
outlets perverse.
Questions reverberate,
stimulate trauma
undermining violence,
wrongfully x-ing
youthful zest.

Becoming Nonbinary

A transgender person can legally change now.
People can change their sex to nonbinary.
For many people such choice somehow
releases opportunity–extraordinary.
> Gender is a spectrum, some state.
> Female or male? Some don't relate.

People can change their sex to nonbinary.
No longer defined by their biology.
They can concentrate on what's primary.
They can include their psychology.
> Perhaps some discrimination will stop–
> not about between your legs or shape on top.

For many people such choice somehow
removes barriers to jobs, driving, records
asking sex identity even health care– to allow
lives to be lived freely without limiting words.
> Cultures often assign gender roles,
> create separations, restrict goals.

Releases opportunities–extraordinary
it has taken this long to be more inclusive.
Why do labels have to be customary
or have to be so exclusive?
> We are all people with supposed sentience
> trying to live an earthly experience.

Gender is a spectrum, some state.
We could be at extremes or in between.
The criteria is open to debate.
Identity documents are used to screen
> who gets what and access.
> Gender equality could be a success.

Female or male? Some don't relate.
They could be asexual or gender neutral.
You need a head and heart to create
a society where respect and kindness are central.
> I'm a feminist supporting a nonbinary choice
> for anyone needing a stronger voice.

World Naked Bike Ride
   Portland, Oregon

The World Naked Bike Ride is a protest
against our dependence on oil
and for cyclist safety. But why naked?

I guess some oil in clothes,
snarls gas-guzzling traffic,
draws attention to causes.

10,000 people jiggle 9.5 miles,
stop for food, music, exhibits, games;
loop smoothly, swiftly through town.

Participators and spectators view
the road hogging and clogging
as annoyers and voyeurs.

Some fear lewd conduct, violence,
unwanted physical contact,
inconvenience of bottlenecks.

Police shut down streets
to let the nude mass pass.
Sometimes confrontations result.

Occasionally a driver will crash
through, to cross past horde--
in a hurry or to get closer view?

Bicyclists don't cross train tracks,
avoid steep hills, several bridges,
though Tilikum Crossing is designed for them.

Bikers prefer wide streets,
but not freeway ramps to funnel
thousands of activists through town.

Organizers can't reveal the route
publicly for safety. Sneak-peekers
could line parade route with camp chairs.

I applaud the causes, but protest method?
I'm not a biker, looker, or car rider while
the naked cyclists shake things up.

Responsible Rebels

Historically, women have not been validated or represented by the models of traditional religion that have frequently been used to establish and validate male hierarchy, power, control of the people, stifle creative thought and provide a moral imperative for obliterating those who dissent or believe differently. Many religions also ask us to relinquish responsibility for our lives, surrendering to a "Higher Power" or to those who claim to be God's messengers. Amber Coverdale Sumrall and Patrice Vecchione

In this time of the surging feminine
old power structures are crumbling.
New ways of believing can determine
what old ways will be tumbling.
>   Get up off your knees.
>   Stand tall for what frees.

Old power structures are crumbling.
Inequities are challenged, rejected.
Rigid leaders are stumbling,
as people are reconnected.
>   See what needs to be done.
>   The revolution has begun.

New ways of believing can determine
what injustices must be addressed.
No longer the control of the masculine,
can be allowed by the oppressed.
>   Politics, Big Business, religion
>   need to bring new voices in.

What old ways will be tumbling?
What will be the discussions?
Many people will be grumbling.
What will be the repercussions?
>   Can change come with peace?
>   Will discrimination cease?

Get up off your knees.
You don't lift up looking at the ground.
Do you need a deity to please?
Are you willing to look around?
>   Open blocks to your thinking.
>   A new world is brinking.

Stand tall for what frees.
Sustain souls and our planet.
Regressive Institutions and committees
failed. The future is ours- so plan it.
>   We must take action, eject the status quo.
>   But don't do it just because anyone told you so.

Future Shock

We must search out totally new ways to anchor ourselves, for all the old
roots–religion, nation, community, family, profession–are now shaking
under the hurricane impact of the accelerative thrust.   Alvin Toffler

Futurist Alvin Toffler, was a post-industrial age guru.
He saw manufacturing and mass production economy shift.
Traumatic upheavals will bring more hopeful story, he knew
computerized, informational-based model could uplift.
　　　He pronounced the downfall of old, centralized hierarchy.
　　　Is a dispersed and responsive society–just malarkey?

He saw manufacturing and mass production economy shift.
We could bring culture and future shocks in the process.
Life's accelerating pace and changes leave some adrift,
overturn relationships, protests covered in the press.
　　　He and others offer wide-ranging predictions.
　　　Who will proffer their prescriptions?

Traumatic upheavals will bring more hopeful story, he knew
we could live underwater, found space colonies-- frontiers
of spirit could increase prosperity and well-being–but who
will take care of our land and water, remove hierarchical tiers?
　　　We must think through what's attainable
　　　to see if the shockwave is sustainable.

Computerized, information-based model could uplift
communication, discoveries, our human body.
Information overload on a chip. Gaps could cause a rift.
Is everything reduced to a commodity?
　　　A hybrid of producer with consumer
　　　becomes a populace of "the prosumer"?

He pronounced the downfall of old centralized hierarchy
with exclusions, wealth imbalances, opportunity gaps.
Can we escape greed, inequities, war's anarchy?
Can we escalate changes without catastrophic collapse?
　　　All of our interactive media, electronic devices
　　　present a world that repels and entices.

Is a dispersed and responsive society–just malarkey?
A pipe-dream before a nightmare?
Are we looking into the future lens too darkly
not knowing what light we will find there?
　　　Nature and space can cause us adversity.
　　　High-tech cannot protect all diversity.

Lost in the Clouds

Ancient Discoveries

Human knowledge has been changing
from the word go
and people in certain aspects
behave more rationally
than they did
when they didn't have it.
They spend less time
doing rain dances
and more time
seeding clouds.

Herbert Stein

Multi-traumatized Species
Multi-traumatized species: Barbara Hand Clow term

As a result of a catastrophe about 11,500 years ago
there were few survivors, civilizations lost.
Other extinctions we are beginning to know,
a multi-traumatized species is the cost.
> Are we wounded healers awakening?
> This current unstable world is shaking.

There were few survivors, civilizations lost.
Survivors struggled to reseed
from a cosmic cataclysmic holocaust,
leaving messages for us to heed.
> No wonder we have ooparts
> from the remainders and new starts.

Other extinctions we are beginning to know.
Most cultures talk of the global flood,
the result of comet fragments melting ice flow,
leaving residues of blood and mud.
> But that is just one incident we speculate about.
> We have had other extinctions of equal clout.

A multi-traumatized species is the cost.
Perhaps why we exist with such violence and fear?
How many resources will we exhaust?
Our murky future appears unclear.
> New technology tools are finding
> our current understanding isn't binding.

Are we wounded healers awakening
supposedly seeking higher dimensional solutions?
Away from dark- light, judgment-control making
choices for heart-filled, unconditional love resolutions.
> Though our species' past has been horrendous,
> perhaps our future can be stupendous.

This current unstable world is shaking,
from pollution, land shifts, surface drilling
radiation, lava-flowing, earthquaking.
What prophesy are we fulfilling?
> Destructive upheaval? Kindness? Loving peace?
> Can we choose what to live with, what to release?

Rediscoveries of Our Past

With our better technology--
        new history.

We find more clues, strange odd ooparts,
        ancient restarts.

Sentient beings seeded long ago--
        older now know.

Discoveries foreshadow, show
how our species changed to advance.
Revelations given a chance.
New history, ancient restarts, older now know.

Ancient Bones
Cancer found in 1.7 million year old foot and 2 million year old vertebrae hominid ancestor.

Ancient ancestors had some tumors.
Rumors

cancer was from modern life style.
It's been awhile.

Early on our family tree
weren't cancer free.

Perhaps through human history.
cancer tumors grew within us--
voracious and insidious.
Rumors its been awhile. Weren't cancer free.

Enheduanna: Poet Priestess

2285-2250 BCE Sumerian: En-chief Priestess, hedu-ornament, Ana of Heaven. Works: The Great-Hearted Mistress, The Exaltation of Inanna, Goddess of the Fearsome Powers.

First author's work found by name,
set the style for poetry.
Her prayers, psalms and poems acclaim
Goddess Innanna, the deity.

She wrote forty liturgical works
copied for over 2000 years.
Model for Bible psalms and Greeks
and other cultures it appears.

The hopes and fears of everyday life
written in a temple to Innana.
She's a priestess, god Nanar's wife,
King Sargon's daughter named Enheduanna.

A woman of great power lived in Ur.
In charge of a temple in her day.
Paradigms of poetry from this writer
still part of poetry today.

Her image was found on a disc
with her hairdresser and her scribe Sagadu.
Somehow makes memory crisp,
her story seem personal and true.

How many writers' works were lost through time?
Perhaps preserved in Akashic Records?
How many writers would prime
new viewpoints, promote concords?

The influence of Enheduanna lasts,
passed on through challenges of time.
Her prowess and creativity casts
hope for the future of poetry and rhyme.

Pierian Persian

> Longest poem by single poet, the Shahnameh contains 62 stories, 990 chapters, 60,000 rhyming couplets. Written for 33 years until 1010 AD by Ferdowsi.

Persian culture's mythology,
> verse anthology

contains heroes, love, history
> saves mystery,

revives past before invasions,
> keeps occasions.

National epic of Persians,
revered today as masterpiece,
for justice, truth, order and peace.
Verse anthology saves mystery, keeps occasions.

Updating the Shahnameh

I have revived the Ajam with my verse
For I have spread the seed of the word.
Whoever has sense, path and faith
After my death will send me praise.
                    Ferdowsi–Poet of the Shahnameh

The longest poem by single poet in the world:
the Shahnameh by Persian poet Ferdowsi.
Poem took 33 years before unfurled
in 1010 AD preserving ancient Persian mystery.
          Seven volumes with 60,000 rhyming couplets,
          serving mythical, heroic and historical outlets.

The Shahnameh by Persian poet Ferdowsi
urges us to avoid evil to strive for virtue.
The poem's slanted toward the vision of a "he",
and preserves a Zoroastrian point of view.
          Also called "The Book of Kings".
          I'd like to hear more feminine side of things.

Poem took 33 years before unfurled
and delivered to Sultan Mahmud of Ghazni.
A Persian poetic masterpiece, so praises swirled
among a very masculine, hierarchical historiography.
          A National Persian epic still today,
          holding many generations in its sway.

In 1010 AD preserving ancient Persian mystery
was important after an Islamic Caliphate age.
He consulted prose and poetry sources diligently
to rescue and revive language, culture, heritage.
          He was a well-educated, wealthy, noble dehgan,
          from land owners and community leaders in Iran.

Seven volumes with 60,000 rhyming couplets
of exquisite, moving, superb quality,
to uplift morals, learn from mistakes, and not forget.
His name means from paradise–fardisi.
          Seven times longer than Homer's Iliad.
          I wonder about the lives women had?

Serving mythical, heroic, and historical outlets,
written from a now ancient, privileged voice.
Now we've turned new pages, more technical gadgets.
We can record more poetic wisdom with wider choice.
          Enough of long-winded tomes of history
          I'm ready for an epic kavi about shestory.

Time Shifting

After writing a poem about smartphone-app Pokeman Go,
I researched nine dimensions and lost civilizations.
There are so many new discoveries I do not know.
My curiosity brings many fascinating realizations.
    Input overload led me to take a nap.
    I experienced some time overlap.

I researched the nine dimensions and lost civilizations,
but when I fell asleep it seemed like Connecticut 1958.
My father took me to an appointment with expectations
I would call for pick up. But I had no phone to operate.
    I was agile, energetic and ended up walking to Hartford,
    saw no phone booth, blithely wandered. Nothing to board.

There are so many new discoveries I do not know.
In the dream I skipped down stairs of a department store,
behind a stage putting on some kind of show.
There was an extensive interior mall beyond the door.
    Glittering shops until I walked outside.
    A gray cold city spread far and wide.

My curiosity brings many fascinating realizations.
This view had icicles hanging from concrete--
like stalactites on parking garage levels' foundations.
An elderly couple, she in a wheelchair greet
    me and answer my question. It's 3054.
    I'm not in summery 2016 Oregon anymore.

Input overload led me to take a nap,
to time shift from past to present and future.
My Dad's been dead decades, I've still no app.
I have aging, arthritic knees to nurture.
    I see changes in mobility and shades of light.
    Sparkles of gold on eyelids made waking bright.

I experienced some time overlap,
lapses in connection and communication.
I returned to present time in a snap.
Was it a dream or hallucination?
    I liked feeling so adept
    and the spritely way I stepped.

In the "Cloud"

Dealing with Technology

Although we leave traces
of our personal lives
with our credit cards
and web browsers,
tomorrow's mobile devices
will broadcast clouds
of personal data
to invisible monitors
all around us.

Howard Rheingold

Keeping Up with the OED

The Oxford English Dictionary
updates four times a year.
My paper dictionary is so far behind.
I'll have to upgrade my word-herd
and find definitions on-line.

As a word-player, word-lover,
I eagerly peruse the new list:
Yolo and Yoda, moobs and biatch,
cheese eater, clickbait, squee, vom,
fuhgeddaboudit, shoppertainment,
uh-oh, non-apology, upspeak,
witching hour, 'Merica selected.
I have lots of word-probing on-line to do.

Some words are Dahlesque
for Roald Dahl's birth centennial,
splendiferous, scrumdiddlyumptious,
Oompa Loompa, human bean.
These playful words will be fun to rhyme.

But all the words I have missed
that delightfully exist are mind-blowing.
So many words hard to find in books.
How do I find all the words I lack?
It will be splendiferous to find out.

Off the Page
The asterisk has become an exclamation point.   Michele Norris

The asterisk * is a star-shaped figure used in printing to indicate
an omission or reference to a footnote.
An exclamation point ! is a punctuation mark used after
a sudden forceful utterance or interjection.
Off the page in this digital age we see the intentions
behind expressions on the screen, off the record or in person.

The Presidential Election 2016 sees candidates
bellowing exclamations with many assertions--
asterisk, either should have been omitted
or misleading lacking documentation.
Fact checkers peruse their screens and pages
to see what is true, false, just inappropriate.

Will either be an asterisk or an exclamation point
during their term of office? A question mark?
I hope the term dashes-- by following a > period.
The underlining issues must be addressed
not held in (parentheses). Equal sign = needed.
Too many "quotation marks" with little said.

An asterisk could roll into action;
an exclamation mark tipped to slash /.
A % of the population is undecided
& @ voter needs to look beyond $'s
and ^ sense in their selection. Use #
responsibly in social media + personal contact.

Trump/despot blathers and sniffs offensive
comments; lacks plans for anything but groping.
Clinton/female partner suffers trust issues
due to emails and husband's conduct.
The libertarian/ill-informed does not know Aleppo.

In the future will they imprint as * or ! ... or interabang

Interabangs

Nonstandard punctuation mark used in written languages and intended to combine the functions of the question mark and the exclamation mark and point, indicating a mixture of query and interjection. Dictionary.com

Shortly after "The Big Bang",
Cosmic Planners exclaimed "Hot Dang".
     The universe starts an interabang.

Presidential candidates debate as polls swang
and one continues to harangue,
     Listeners hear an interabang.

The terror 9/11 when planes wizard prang,
or when Florence Foster Jenkins sang,
     witnesses express an interabang.

But pianist Lang Lang
fashion designer Vera Wang
     elicit an enthusiastic interabang.

Crowded, riding straphang
a jolt, a sudden stop brang
     surprise, a use for an interabang.

Riding in or on a mustang,
or dodging a boomerang
     brings an exuberant interabang.

When a beast reveals its fang,
or anti-gang interfaces a gang,
     heart pumps an interabang.

Actions of Batman and Superman's intergang–
comic characters wield metal clang.
     Imagination on interabang.

Watching a prisoner hang
or mother's childbirth pang
     requires an interabang.

Under a broken branch of a zamang--
a dangerous, storm-tossed overhang--
     watcher shrieks an interabang.

Clutching heart as young child up-swang,
or anxious as measles outsprang,
        brings parents to interabang.

Wondering if the Zika virus stang
turns knees and stomach to meringue,
        waiting churns an interabang.

Caught between yin and yang
or in chess–zugzwang–
        a tough spot for interabang.

When the phone call never rang
or when a romance lost its tang
        you feel an interabang.

Puzzling urban slang
or some dialect's twang
        elicits an interabang

Firefang, parasang, saladang, quandang, kiang,
trepang, alang, chang, orang, lang, vang
        are unfamiliar words rhyming with interabang.

Spelled interrobang or interabang, term sprang
from question mark and exclamation point-- they upsprang.
        with shared dot –now interabang.

I'd have to be a whizzbang
to be able to be amang
        all the ways for us to interabang

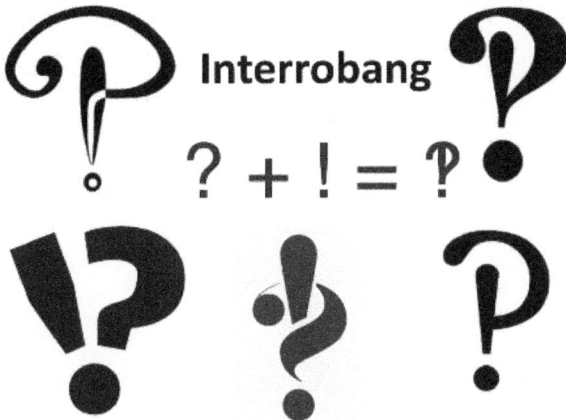

Interrobang

$$? + ! = ?$$

Reading Closed Books

I think it is almost inevitable that terahertz imaging will be an important technology in numerous future applications. Daniel Mittleman

A high- tech terahertz spectrometer can
read a closed book with a radiation scan
on electromagnetic spectrum between
microwaves and infrared light, see unseen
contents of old books too fragile to handle,
examine painting for authenticity and avoid scandal,
can understand an artist's creative process,
found hidden face behind Roman fresco with success.
They can analyze mummies, peek through an envelope
with a gizmo–a cross between camera and microscope.

X-rays can damage documents and art–its limitation.
This system uses ultra-short bursts of terahertz radiation.
The device is a long way from reading an entire book.
But someday they'll be few places it can't look.

His New Smart Phone

Techno-nerd (husband) and techno-phobic-word (me)
while driving home between storms from Portland,
we wrestle with smart phone technology.
Neither of us see clearly or fully understand.
>   The phone gets caught inside his sport's vest,
>   prompting a brouhaha, unsportsman-like contest.

While driving home between storms from Portland
the infernal phone would ring intermittently,
but out of his reach or at his command.
His jostling and tussling was frustrating me.
>   Trying to drive, he struggled to free it.
>   One-handed, he pried pocket to see it.

We wrestle with small smart phone technology.
I do not even have push-button cell phone.
His new phone operates by touch apparently.
Frantically we both fumble-finger, bumble-prone.
>   When he retrieved it, the caller's name was unseen,
>   for he wore no near-glasses to view the screen.

Neither of us see clearly or fully understand
how nimble fingers are supposed to swish.
Light flashes and flutters when we demand
some response to strategy for what we wish.
>   I had no idea where to place a finger.
>   Fickle messages would not linger.

The phone gets caught inside his sport's vest,
then he hands it to clueless me to hold.
No pushing keys, so though I try my best
I do not connect or do what I'm told.
>   As we shout instructions, somehow daughter hears.
>   At a red light we learn of her fears.

Prompting a brouhaha, unsportsman-like contest
she interprets our confusion as we were in danger.
At the red light we finally hear her request.
Our smart phone remains a source of our anger.
>   If I'm to be phone manager when he's driving,
>   until I'm smarter coach–many time outs when riding.

Pokeman Go

Pokeman Go has arrived in our valley.
The smartphone-app with virtual creatures leads
people off their couches to exercise really
fulfilling interactive and playful needs.
>Going globally viral, the pocket monster hunt,
>Pokemon Go has obstacles to confront.

The smartphone-app with virtual creatures leads
all ages by GPS to proceed in actual reality,
to catch Pokemon while a loved one pleads
to look out where the player goes...safely.
>Some play when riding in a car,
>but when driving they go too far.

People off their couches to exercise really
multi-task as they play with realities and run.
Sometimes they stop and talk, actually
sharing their free game and their fun.
>Squirtle, Pikachu, Jigglepuff go too
>on a new playing field with a different crew.

Fulfilling interactive and playful needs,
people get distracted, don't pay attention.
They can go to dangerous areas, no one heeds
until casualty found in unknown location.
>There are some places players should not go–
>places off limits, private places players should know.

Going globally viral, the pocket monster hunt
creates lure-a-thons, pub crawls and "hot spots".
To find more Pokemon to affront,
a place to become hot shots.
>Bringing people together is good,
>if they play carefully as they should.

Pokemon Go has obstacles to confront.
Players' lives are literally in their hands.
I'll not be performing the Pokeman Go stunt.
I have no mobile device to give commands.
>I have to depend on what I see,
>try to keep my mind and hands free.

Bogging Down on Blogs

The presenter with her Powerpoints
illuminates the screen with splashes
of images, color, words of insight.
We are to approach a blog like a magazine,
have a sense of purpose and years
of ideas to run with.

A blog is a reverse diary with recent entries
first and past entries archived.
We develop a community connected
around an idea, create a voice
for getting out news, a playground
for creative projects, a brand,

a space for an online presence. I guess.
Facebook is social media. Instagram
is more visual with captions. Websites,
Twitter, Tinder, Tumblr etc. I'm slogged down
before I even create a blog. I don't know
any of these, no cell phone, use e-mail.

The presenter has five blogs for different areas.
For her a blog is a structure and the blogger
needs to write one sentence what the blog is about
to hook the person fishing. A Psychographic Profile
becomes more important than Demographics
to lure readers to your site.

We are not short of blogs. Hundreds of thousands
of bloggers are setting goals and trying
to connect with those of similar interests.
A blogger's job is to make readers care about you.
She lists 21 different kinds of blogs which
you should add to at least once a month.

My hand tires of taking notes when she says
they are on her blog, so we don't need to take notes.
How to set up a blog is beyond this presentation.
Websites and blogs will take you through the steps.
She says there is blogging fatigue. Keep fresh.
I'm too bogged down to blog...to start.

Scams Scram

Another scam caller squawking,
Another product they're hawking.
Another service I don't need.
Another threat I'll not heed.

Robo-calls about my computer.
Any time they're an intruder.
Early and late calls, during rest,
work, play, they try their best.

Sometimes an unpaid IRS
or someone dear is in a mess.
I missed jury duty and must pay up
despite off the list to show up.

Bring money to a certain location
or police will come is provocation.
Some calls ring and no one's there.
Some calls require sheriff made aware.

When I am watching TV
the caller is identified for me.
But some callers say anonymous,
so don't get picked up by us.

Our answer machine picks up many.
But scam calls—I don't want any!
A call! I don't know whose talking.
Let it ring. Leave message. I'm balking.

I've debated about getting a cell phone.
Will the scammers leave me alone?
My husband says it might be worse.
So, I'll hang up and bluntly rehearse.

Ads on TV and on-line
They waste time and I decline.
Some days communicating seems over-rated.
I'll not up-grade. I remain agitated.

Scamming the Scammer

"Hello my name is Steve.
I am calling about your computer...".

"Oh, so glad you called.
Perhaps you can answer my questions
about my computer. You sound nice.
Is that an Indian accent? Asian?
Can you help me from so far away?
Worth a try. I'm really flummoxed.
My grandson could not figure out
my printer lines and poor colors.
I just cannot figure out
what all the computer keys,
all the symbols and files do.
Just when I have figured
out how to copy a file to email,
my finger slips and it does not
transfer and I start again.
My husband says I should make
attachments, but I cannot
get the sequence right.
Then there is clipping parts
of things to put elsewhere
and darned if I know how
to do that. Then there is
deleting hundreds of files.
So tedious! I get a finger cramp.
More irritating is deleting a file by error.
Once I got abort. Abort what?
Sometimes it won't turn on or off
because of updates–takes forever.
How do I start Facebook, Twitter, blog?
Trying to save a file gets
complicated and starting a new one
means a real hassle. Then
sometimes the computer does not
want to send or receive emails--
freezes or something. My friend Vera

has her grandchildren help her, but
she still gets confused and even pros
do not help, but I hope you might be able to.
My husband says I should experiment
and discover what things do.
He says I can't break it
–but I end up doing something
he can't figure out what I did.
Hang on– I'll go ask him what it was I
did last night....."

Leave phone off the hook about
half an hour. Leave Steve hanging.

Hacking

Hacking emails causes political turmoil.
The public is getting hacked also.
Government agencies beginning to roil.
The public is feeling whacked's blow.
> Privacy invaded.
> Everyone's jaded.

The public is getting hacked also.
Social media chose what to share.
Selfies of things we need not know,
displaying images everywhere.
> Someone's decoding us all
> causing a folderol.

Government agencies beginning to roil
blaming Russia, China, insiders.
Security breaches embroil.
Knowledge given to outsiders.
> Digital information taken
> leaves everyone shaken.

The public is feeling whacked's blow.
Private parts on cell and computer
come back to haunt, will never go,
remain a constant intruder.
> Whatever is allowed
> remains in the Cloud.

Privacy invaded.
Watch what you post.
Images paraded.
Follow you like a ghost.
> With no social media or cell,
> I escape a private hell?

Everyone's jaded.
Digital age holds all in its fingers.
Everyone's aided
but some negativity lingers.
> If I keep my emails clean.
> I don't care what they glean.

Viv

*Viv is an artificial intelligence program that enables developers to create an
intelligent conversational interface to anything.*

Dag Kittlau, the Siri creator invented Viv,
the next shift in human-computer interaction.
More of what technology can give
to the digitalized generation.
> I am not techno-prone.
> I don't own a cell phone.

The next shift in human-computer interaction
is nearing completion- eagerly awaited.
Viv will be a virtual system sensation.
Siri's query accuracy has been debated.
> Viv will be a chatty gal–
> an advanced AI pal.

More of what technology can give
is to breathe life in inanimate objects
through conversation. Let them live,
intelligently discuss many subjects.
> If all has consciousness and energy,
> I will try this new synergy.

To the digital generation
hooked to fingering, poking screens,
they can talk more, begin veneration
for new AI system for Siri has-beens.
> Since I am not the best typist, I rejoice,
> I can express myself with my voice.

I am not tech-prone.
No skype–just land line.
I am sure I'm not alone
thinking Viv will do just fine.
> For me inanimates always held souls within.
> I collect and respect them to other's chagrin.

I don't own a cell phone,
but might give Viv a try.
Viv appeals to this old crone,
not sure really why.
> Any way people can connect and grow,
> is a system I want to know.

Beyond Human

Nootropics and nanobots could increase life span,
keep us very healthy. Drop a pill,
ingest microscopic cells, nanobots nibble all they can.
Part of us will be human still.
     As we become a transhuman, part robot
     will the soul transfer or not?

Keep us healthy, drop a pill
science is creating miracles.
We will evolve humans until
we are free of earthly cycles.
     Sturdy cyborgs, robotic beings
     can go into space we're foreseeing.

Ingest microscopic cells, nanobots nibble all they can.
Rushing through our blood stream,
they gobble disease, a complete body scan.
A fully functional body is everyone's dream.
     They are also working on a high-tech brain.
     With increased capacity, we will all gain.

Part of us will be human still.
They hope to computerize all knowledge,
input it into everyone's brains, fill
souls and creativity into the collage?
     We will be full of bionic parts.
     Where will people be when this starts?

As we become a transhuman, part robot
we become more adaptable for space.
Fleshy forms tend to rot and clot.
We are a fragile human race.
     If robots go ahead to transplant and terraform
     then extraterrestrial life can become the norm.

Will the soul transfer or not?
How much remains of us in these plans?
How well will we be a polyglot,
with these cosmic clans?
     They are creating more durable, sensitive skin.
     At what point does human end and transhuman begin?

Hello

SETI: Search for Extraterrestial Intelligence Institute
METI: Messaging Extra Terrestrial Intelligence

Earthlings want to chat with space chums say "Hello".
Sitting around waiting for sound signals is SETI.
But scientists want to start sending messages, bellow.
Wanting to send conversation starters is METI.
> They are not sure exactly how to do this.
> Via radio or laser, they still could miss.

Sitting around waiting for sound signals is SETI.
Some say if aliens are hostile do we want to hear?
Are they reclusive like the elusive Yeti?
Perhaps they are avoiding our atmosphere?
> Writer David Brin and Stephen Hawking
> don't want any aliens talking or stalking.

But scientists want to start sending messages, bellow
the perfect message to say "Hello"- a shout out,
but they have not figured out just how
this millions of dollars project will come about.
> Visionaries want to learn and share information,
> to make contact in 2018–this generation.

Wanting to send conversation starters is METI.
Proxima Centauri's rocky planet is their aim.
Calculations more entangled than spaghetti
untangle for more distant destinations for the same
> intentional messages into space,
> targeting stars- "Hi "from the human race.

They are not sure exactly how to do this.
But I believe star stuff, like us came before.
Our alien kin are far from clueless
and if they want could come once more.
> All life is cosmically connected.
> Someday that view will be accepted.

Via radio or laser, they still could miss.
Many people say they are here today.
Perhaps some skeptics still dismiss,
prefer to think if they come, they'll prey.
> Attempts to greet might meet with silence.
> Aliens might not like our violence.

Space Mongers

Space mongers want to explore outer space
for resources, aliens, new home base
for a curious, deleterious, earth-mucking race.

We landed on the moon, but didn't go back.
We're planning on Mars, but a little off track.
A few critical components we still lack.

Pork-barrel politics play a role.
Budgets are hard to control.
But space mongers have a goal.

Tourist and accouterments profits
from landers, rovers, craft and space outfits,
terra-forming gear and maintenance kits.

No exo-planet or planets nearer by
have perfect conditions but why
not give best bets a Star Trek try?

Elon Musk and his SpaceX troops
seem faster at jumping through hoops
and may be first to claim the coups.

Many pundits have suggestions
for where to go and raise questions
with many tantalizing tidbits for digestion.

Largest Saturn moon, nitrogen-air Titan
has methane lakes and clouds that frighten,
cold, good gravity, for some we'll enlighten.

If we adapt there, settlers might don wings,
fly in heavy hydrocarbon air, do things
challenging incredible hardship brings.

If we have destroyed Earth by then
and need a place to start again,
will anywhere be ready? When?

The way we are heading we'd better hop to it,
we have limited time to create and intuit,
perhaps humanity won't live through it.

Beyond Clouds

Exploring the Cosmos

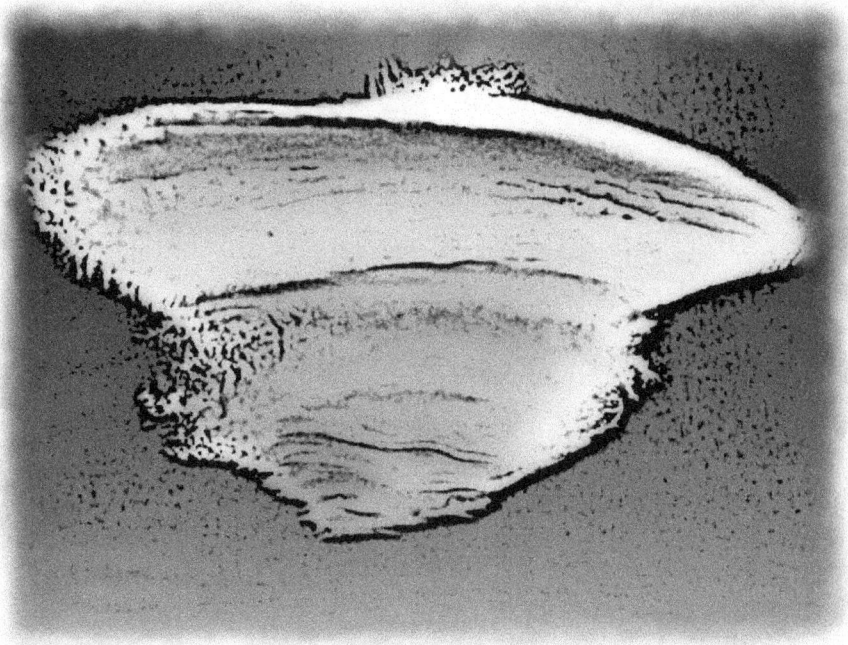

*Stars and planets
were cooked up
as huge clouds
of matter,
collapsed
and coalesced.*

Seth Shostat

A Holographic Universe

> Holograms are 3-D images produced by the interference of light beams
> that reflect off a real, physical object and can be seen with the naked eye.

Some scientists conclude we live
in a holographic universe.
Maybe multiverse, but what source
runs the projector, provides the light?

In the vastness of space
what energy, vibration
controls what is light (or dark),
creates these possible realities.

On Earth reality is viewed
through many lenses-visions, re-visions.
Surreality, virtual reality, imagination,
myriad interpretations and augmented reality.

It is all supposed to be illusion, anyhow.
Other dimensions are without time?
All could be a one-shot, simultaneous
reality show-- we are performer and audience?

We can wear 3-D glasses at the movies,
but now augmented equipment on the job.
Augmented reality glasses display diagrams,
instructional images for quality checks.

More people will wear headgear
for computer processing and optical projections
to create digital holograms that users can see
and interact with in their real environment.

Now with a flip of a finger, a slice of reality
appears in your hand. Change it,
if you prefer another perspective.
Reality flattens on the screen.

I do not have a cell phone, but have computer.
I am fascinated by instant access images,
Hololens is an advanced "mixed reality"--
computer headset users can interact with.

3-D printers are amazing for art and science.
Our holographic universe is really playing
with our hands and minds. So much data!
Whatever universe we have is expanding.

With dreams, multidimensional contacts,
magical reality, imagination and fantasy–
lower tech access to some of these realities,
but they are enhanced by digital realities?

Realities shift beyond my control.
If we shift to 5-D reality, we'll adapt, I guess.
Vibrations supposedly connect everything.
Energy provides the action for reality change.

I confess the high-tech reality is indeed
extraordinary, but for me an elderly
ordinary sort, I get lost trying to keep up.
What realities can I experience?

I want to know about my reality options
even though I have no intention of using them.
Experiencing and imagining realities
anywhere in the cosmos is challenging.

Wonder if I could tweak my hologram
to be younger, more mobile, more intelligent?
If my vibe gets higher, another dimension
might lure my curiosity, enhance my light?

The Strangers

We are all strangers in a strange land, longing for home, but not quite knowing what or where home is. We glimpse it sometimes in our dreams, or as we turn a corner, and suddenly, there is a strange, sweet familiarity, then vanishes almost as soon as it comes.   Madeliene L'Engle

Scientists from many nations discovered
the Vela supercluster- just one of millions
of clusters and galaxies we have found.
Think of all the places in just this universe
which could be our origin! Our soul could
reincarnate multiversally, even simultaneously.

Earth is the current sentient experience
we are aware of, but we dream of others.
Dreams create otherworldly visions.
Maybe other soul-slivers' lives
we get a glimpse of–or parallel lives?
We could be serial strangers.

As for home, home appears temporary--
where we focus on or are conscious of.
Many seek a more warm-fuzzy cosmic home,
living light-bodied in Valhallas or heavens,
where we commune with enlightened beings
designed by a Prime Creator, part of ALL.

Room for many points of views, we lack
consensus how to define home--
in earthly realm only or cosmically.
Strangers seek companions, beings
who resonate on their wave-length.
It is a life-long quest to build a home.

A stranger is unaccustomed, not known before,
unacquainted with oneself and others.
People tend to fear the unknown and different.
I lean toward light- beings of love to share a home.
I'm fascinated by the possibilities of strangeness
and home. I just need to keep the lights on.

Radiant Showers

This abundant year for the Perseid meteors showered
506 in 4.75 hours. 150 in 20 minutes.
The meteors come from a single point,
radiating from the Perseus constellation.
In an elongated orbit we see them when Earth
crosses the orbital path of comet Swift-Tuttle.
This comet rubble dazzles Earthlings
mostly after midnight. Jupiter's gravity
aids these bright, swift streaks,
we see in a 3-5 hour window
after a waxing gibbous moon sets.

Decades ago, visiting my mother in Connecticut
we lounged in lawn chairs, nibbling snacks,
watching the Perseid's display with neighbors,
laughing and searching despite city-light blurred skies.

Now while you wait you can watch Late Night TV
with middle-aged white guys straining to entertain.
But I was enthralled with the Rio Olympics--
the USA women's gymnastics team- The Final Five
showered in gold, bejeweled in starry glitter.

The meteor shower radiates from the Perseus
constellation near the Double Cluster.
This hero's father, Zeus appeared
before his mother Danae in a shower of gold.

But I chose to watch another stellar duo--
Simone Biles and Aly Raisman
rocket across the beam and floor,
radiating their own gold and silver.
Totally forgot to watch the dark sky
and moonset for the Perseids.

I watched Perseid Shower photos on the Internet.
One fast meteor left a light blue smoke trail
lasting 45 seconds. Spectacular, but I had found
a good spot to watch and wait,
showered with delight on my couch.
I gleam witnessing entities
out-shine their surroundings.

Oh, the Places We Can Go!

There are billions of planets in our cosmos capable of sustaining human life.
Where will you go next? Judy Santori

Some speculate our DNA codes come
from several local star systems. Wow!
Activate "dormant" DNA and we're welcome
to vibrations of these star systems somehow.
> Bodies upgraded over time.
> I knew I wasn't at my prime.

From several local star systems? Wow!
Veil of forgetfulness when born? Don't remember?
My last incarnation where? What planetary powwow?
I wonder what cosmic tribe member?
> Most places's frequency: 5th dimensional.
> Was this 3D vibe really intentional?

Activate "dormant" DNA and we're welcome
to adjust to the vibration of love.
Our Earth love goal far from this outcome.
Maybe other beings will give us a shove?
> Supposedly Gaia's frequency is rising.
> We must release hate. Not surprising.

To vibrations of these star systems somehow
requires curiosity and leap of hope.
To other ethics we might bow,
and have other ways to cope.
> Here we create this reality ourselves.
> Elsewhere they create their reality themselves.

Bodies upgraded over time
whether here or elsewhere in space.
Let us sparkle, cleanse the grime.
I long for a light-filled, peaceful place.
> All these experiences return to Source,
> and a Universal Library cosmic resource?

I knew I wasn't at my prime.
I believe I am multidimensional.
I'm living prose, when I want to rhyme.
My service here in provisional.
> I look forward to my next cosmic chance
> and for my functionality to advance.

234

Cosmic Starseeds

Some part of our being knows this is where we came from. We yearn to return. And we can. Because the cosmos is also within us. We're made of star-stuff. We are a way for the cosmos to know itself. Carl Sagan

Cosmic starseeds from other planets
usually are compassionate and loving?
They came to re-experience, to help
those who have forgotten who they are
and where they came from?

The goal of humanity Lars Sarnutt says
is to love everyone even if in your opinion
they don't deserve it and to do no harm
to anyone. (Kind of hard right now.)

Practice saying "I love you
and I respect you even though
I do not resonate with the way you act."
(Another tough one to do with some people.)

We are all connected to every living thing
and the planet. Help the planet heal itself
and raise in vibration together? (Cooperative
connection is currently on trend.)

Apparently we all come from a place of love
even those who choose negative, dominating
and controlling energies? Some seeds don't sprout.
We'll nurture those who grow? Sounds like a plan.

Am I a starseed?   Are you?
Here is a suggested check list.
1. Excel in healing, teaching, the arts
    environmental assistance and social outreach.
2. Empaths–sensitive to energy and other's feelings.
3. Interested in space, nature, science fiction, UFO's,
    crystals, other worlds, ancient cultures, Atlantis and Lemuria.
4. Have a deep longing to fulfill a mission.
5. A feeling of emptiness, homesick.
6. Depression which can trigger awakening.
7. Universal Law makes more sense than Earth Law.

Children born after 1994 have more
than two DNA strands activated?
One of starseed's jobs is to bring
them into this world and be stewards
until they get into their own power.
(They are the future of humanity?)

If we each are a soul-splinter
from the Prime Source sparked
into a form–this time homo sapiens,
we are indeed starseeded from star stuff?

We could be multidimensional,
multi-universal on a cosmic journey
beyond our imagination–just
a starseedlet, energized
for the long haul on a starry trek.

I happen to believe I'm a starseed, who
birthed a starseed, to procreate starseeds.
I choose to believe I have lived on many worlds
and have many otherworldly places to be.
        Curiosity and light lure me onward.

Skylings

Chinese saw a city in the clouds in two locations--
not a Fata Morgana, group hallucination, mass apparition.
People see motherships, have space craft observations.
Governments won't discuss any such cosmic situation.
> These skylings- objects and beings surround us.
> Why do these issues still confound us?

Not a Fata Morgana, group hallucination, mass apparition,
the cloud city scope was beyond a holographic hoax.
Some people record and tell others, petition
to be taken seriously, not butt of jokes.
> Has science fiction prepared us to see
> a vision with a wider cosmic possibility?

People see motherships, have space craft observations,
believe aliens have landed, tweaked our DNA.
They're our guardians? Developers of our civilizations?
We're in a cosmic experiment in which we have little say?
> Our telescopes, radio waves, space craft scans
> still haven't revealed our place in cosmic plans.

Governments won't discuss any such cosmic situation,
even after Roswell and people telling of otherworldly contacts.
Geniuses and psychics with interdimensional conversation
abilities, share information which this connection extracts.
> Such arrogance to think in such vastness we are alone.
> Our limited equipment leaves us ignorance prone.

These skylings- objects and beings surround us
to let us know we are watched and tested.
Does a Prime Directive- choices hound us?
Is our evolution being arrested?
> Do skylings control or protect us?
> Will they accept or reject us?

Why do these issues still confound us?
If we are a part of cosmic creation
why hasn't the Prime Creator's plan found us?
We get inklings, a subliminal sensation–
> but unclouded answers are few.
> Just what are we supposed to do?

Cosmic Fireworks
Who needs fireworks when you have stars? Catie Leary

Every moment thousands or millions of light-years away
beyond our naked eye, but accessible by strong telescopes
specstarcular explosions and implosions burst--
not just for earthbound special celebrations.

Celestial fireworks like a small galaxy Kiso 5639
NASA calls a "tadpole" because its bright head and elongated tail–
a white eye in a red head with sparkly tail.
Tadpoles are rare locally, but more common in the distant cosmos.

The Butterfly Nebula- NGC 6302 in the Scorpius constellation
is wing-like with white within and orange-red edges.
The colorful Crab Nebula, NGC 1952
looks like a rainbow-hued mesh with lots of greens and blues.

UGC 1810 and ARP 273 resemble a rose
with a spiral bloom and wispy stalk.
Herbig-Haro has a three million mile long jet–
a pink and white contrail– somewhat dragon-ish.

Eta Carinas features two stars in cataclysmic explosion.
Bi-lobed, reddish with a white center.
Supernova 198 7A has circular dots
like a pink pearl necklace.

The Ant Nebula- Menzel 3 with firework-like rays
and bursts look like two lightbulbs colliding.
Puppis Constellation NGC 2440 is one of the hottest
white dwarf stars blurs red, white and blue.

Daily I can gaze at the twinkling, sparkly stars
if the clouds do not obscure my view,
but I know they are there, not temporarily
like the patriotic displays on July 4th holiday.

Stellar Fireworks
Who needs fireworks when you have stars. Catie Leary

Cosmic outbursts specstarcular–
        awesome, stellar.

Supernovas, stars, galaxies
        Milky way–see

with-without telescope, scan sky.
        Nebulous–why?

Shapes like dragon or butterfly.
Stars form mythic constellations,
in spiral configurations–
awesome, stellar Milky Way–see nebulous–why?

Gravitational Wave Music

Echoes of two crashing black holes--
music for souls.

Second is a higher pitch chirp
like angel's harp?

Sounds like jazz, classical music--
a cosmic trick?

Soundtrack becomes the bailiwick
of scientists new instruments.
Song from outer space augments
music for souls like an angel harp, a cosmic trick.

Asteroids

Asteroids supposedly life-seeded Earth
from very ancient times.
Now assessed for mineral worth
as we seek cosmic climes.
  We think asteroids can be for our benefit.
  We want to penetrate their orbit.

From very ancient times
asteroids brought elements to create life.
All the ingredients to prime
asteroids to become Earth's midwife.
  We are all star stuff.
  We can't thank asteroids enough.

Now assessed for mineral worth,
probes even found water.
Will colonies and factories berth
in the asteroid belt's backwater?
  Using materials from asteroids
  we'll venture unto cosmic voids?

As we seek cosmic climes
for escape routes from Earth changes,
places without unsustainable rimes
for possible residence exchanges.
  Asteroids are stepping stones
  to exploit while Gaia groans.

We think asteroids can be for our benefit,
forget they can smash us to smithereens.
If unstopped, we may get cataclysmically hit,
onslaught witnessed on our digital screens.
  Might cramp our ability to explore,
  as humanity could be no more.

We want to penetrate their orbit,
land a notch in the asteroid belt,
share surreal estate. Can we fit?
Quite bumpy, clumpy. I have felt
  possibly they have performed their mission
  to seed us, perhaps put us out of commission?

Naming the Cosmos

Stars, moons, planets, galaxies, constellations--
they have intriguing non-hybrid, number/letter names.
But exo-planets have hybrid designations
I'd like to see more individual, original naming aims.
      I just discovered Mars stars Zubeneschamali
      in Libra Constellation with Zubenelgenubi.

They have more intriguing non-hybrid, number/letter names
but now the discoveries in space are compounding.
Billions of objects can't get even nicknames
as rate of nomenclature needs is astounding.
      We could keep pace with naming exo-planets so far.
      I am dazzled by the names found for a star.

But exo-planets have hybrid designations
so distant, clinical and unappealing.
Even space craft are named with destinations.
Exo-planet beings could have names they're concealing.
      Let's think beyond scientists and myth.
      Think of new names we are excited with.

I'd like to see more individual, original naming aims.
There are many languages we can choose from.
Globally astronomers and citizens could make their claims.
Let's become more linguistically adventuresome.
      Perhaps people could give names for an exo-planet
      like they have for stars. Select one from Internet?

I just discovered Mars stars Zubeneschmali.
I scoured star name lists and star's meaning.
Alscella, Mira, Arrakis, Rigel, Enif, Prijipati--
any of their essences are we gleaning?
      Sabik, Antares, Mira, Merope, Merope, Alcyone,
      Mothallah, Alcor, Zaniah, Markab, Pherkab, Pleione.

In Libra Constellation with Zubenelgenubi--
Antares and Spica are in constellations nearby.
But exo-planets, just because they are a newbie
gives us a chance to give awesome names a try.
      We could ask any Earthlings to suggest stellar ideas,
      to forward to exo-planet namers by myriad medias.

Albireo: Beta Cygni

Double star called Albireo,
like a shadow.

in the Cygnus constellation.
Contemplation:

what's it like to be double star?
Gazed from afar,

I wonder how stellar you are.
One blue and one gold star duo,
I follow you and want to know
like a shadow. Contemplation, gazed from afar.

Juno and Jupiter

NASA is sending spacecraft Juno to Jupiter
within 3,100 miles of Jupiter's cloud tops.
Juno, Jupiter's mythic cloud-piercing wife
wants to see what is going on.

Jupiter is a world of swirling storms,
dazzling auroras–best in solar system,
dust rings, maybe water, full of gases.
Not sure if there is any rock to stand on.

Juno wants to take a twenty month sneak peak.
This curiosity costs $1.1 billion.
Can Jupiter give us more understanding
of how Earth and solar system developed?

Of Jupiter's numerous moons, we think Europa
might have an ocean under icy surface.
Europa is a target for possible escape routes
when Earth is no longer a viable home.

In Roman mythology Juno was Jupiter's queen,
sister and wife who protected woman and state.
Juno gave birth to Mars and Vulcan while
Jupiter birthed Minerva from top of his head.

The namesake reunion of planet and probe
hopefully will be a fruitful one.
Bright light shows, fast-spins, closer scans
for water, lure us to heftiest, perhaps first planet.

Billowy, mysterious clouds, shroud surface,
a gigantic gas ball of hydrogen and helium,
glowing yellow likely formed after sun,
barged into by Juno after Galileo circled.

Juno's mission is to peer through Jupiter's
cloud-socked atmosphere to map the interior
from vantage point above the poles.
How much water? Why lights so bright?

Interesting questions, possible applications
eventually for people-aggravated problems.
Nature and space elements could eliminate us,
but until then we must maintain Earth and inhabitants.

Following Juno

After Juno traveled almost two billion miles
over five years for a rendezvous,
only one second late to scientists' smiles,
Jupiter and moons appear in clearer view.
>   For twenty months the Juno probe,
>   watches for clouds to disrobe.

Over five years for a rendezvous
takes skill, persistence and patience.
Galileo spacecraft provide a preview
urging further NASA space science.
>   How many resources to put into space?
>   How much for Earth's terrestrial race?

Only one second late to scientists' smiles–
such precision is astounding.
Anxious to proceed so data compiles,
fingers crossed and hearts pounding.
>   Now we play the waiting game.
>   Our vision will never be the same.

Jupiter and moons appear in clearer view.
We hope to increase our understanding
of solar system and Earth's purview
as universe and knowledge are expanding.
>   I am content to wait and watch
>   to see if cosmos has escape hatch.

For twenty months the Juno probe
will map and test elements of planet.
Is it only gaseous, have rock, microbes?
We hope Jupiter has some solids like granite.
>   We need footings–perhaps on a moon
>   for space travelers to even maroon.

Watches for clouds to disrobe
from images relayed to Earth
are examined from astronomers around the globe.
In Jupiter's orbit, Juno's berth
>   could answer questions of Creation
>   with results from cosmic cooperation.

Starry Treks

Fifty years since Star Trek
would boldly go into the space frontier
with utopian imagination, great stories,
diverse cast and high tech gear.

Many devices are now in use,
we are probing further into space.
Yet, Earth appears threatened, dystopian,
with many challenges for the human race.

My imagination explored space
creating scenarios of my own,
which I drew and wrote about as a child.
I've watched to see how far we've flown.

Science and spirituality takes me stellar.
Exo-planets, Dern and Dal universes,
multiple dimensions, guardians, avatars,
alien beings, heralded in many verses.

One intuitive said I travel with the stars
in a space ship to a mothership
to learn about my earthbound role.
I could use a multidimensional tip.

I long for Star Trek's possible future
with respect, tolerance, less conflict.
Several E.T. groups send proposals
how we can upgrade and uplift.

Some starry-eyed optimists
suggest a Fifth Dimensional shift,
DNA- tweaking, an enlightened grid.
Otherworldly beings give us a gift.

A chance to join other cosmic beings--
no longer the backward ones on galactic fringe,
to create a healed world of unity and freedom,
where no controllers can impinge.

Our equipment needs repair and re-visioning,
increased capacity to be celestial in spirit
while manifesting in a low-vibe frequency
would require an illuminating growth spurt.

Explosion of Exoplanets

What a stellar time to be an astronomer–hurray!
Kepler K2 Mission found more exoplanets–yes!
They may be rocky, cool enough- okay!
Over 2400 new worlds so far they guess.
>   Four exo-planets potentially like Earth!
>   Telescopes are proving their worth.

Kepler K2 Mission found more exoplanets–yes!
Before red dwarfs were left out, excluded.
K2 increased its scope and inclusiveness,
now cooler, smaller, brighter red dwarfs are included.
>   Red dwarfs are more common than sun-like stars
>   in the Milky Way, by factor of 20- spectacular!

They may be rocky, cool enough–okay
to host our carbon-based, fleshy fragile kind.
Plenty of opportunities near and far away?
A more peaceful planet beckons my mind.
>   If we are all the sentience there is–
>   the multiverse is an empty abyss.

Over 2400 new worlds so far they guess
and they are really just getting started.
Billions and billions of galaxies express
light and await new explorations-- departed
>   and new missions yet to come.
>   I wonder if we'll be welcome.

Four exo-planets potentially like Earth
20-50% larger with orbits of 5 1/2 - 24 days.
Two have radiation levels to provide berth,
accommodate conditions for earthly stays.
>   I'll name them for the Four Musketeers.
>   I forget their names--until recall appears.*

Telescopes are proving their worth.
Soon James Webb space telescope will expand discoveries.
Astronomy is doubling, tripling mission's girth,
will measure exoplanet's mass, atmospheric qualities.
>   Earth-based telescopes' exo-planet count: 104.
>   Kepler space telescope: 197 current score.

* Four Musketeers: D' Artagnan, Porthos, Aramis, Athos

Proxima b

An Earth-sized planet named Proxima b
orbits the red dwarf star Proxima Centauri.
Our pale-blue dot meets a pale red dot
seemingly in a habitable zone spot.

4.2 light years away this nearest stellar neighbor
is in a Goldilocks Zone which can harbor
liquid water and is not too hot or too cold.
Perhaps some cosmic chums to behold?

Proxima b has orange sky displays,
circles planet for a year in 11 days.
One side stares at sun, other half darkness.
We have no idea the extent of starkness.

We have no idea about the atmosphere,
so no concept of what could be here.
We need an Earth or space telescope
until we comprehend Proxima b's scope.

We think it is small, rocky planet,
but do not take Earth-like for granted.
It may be able to hold its liquid,
but our data is far from solid.

Scientist from eight countries studied the wiggle
the star's light caused by seesaw gravitational wriggle.
Direct observation is not possible with current technology,
so expect speculation and some new mythology.

A visit is around 25 trillion miles away.
New technology is underway.
New Horizons went to Pluto and took a decade,
that's 3 billion miles. More progress needs to be made.

Looking for life on Proxima-b comes next.
Proxies living there might be perplexed,
as to why we have come from so far away
and hope we do not plan to stay.

A Planet with Three Suns

Sunrise-sunset, sunrise-sunset, sunrise-sunset
every day for part of year. Sometimes non-stop daylight.
A year is half a millennium long since onset.
How can a calendar keep things right?
    HD 131399Ab in Constellation Centaurus--
    this planet holds many mysteries before us.

Every day for part of year. Sometimes non-stop daylight--
just fifth triple star system found. This is the biggest orbit.
This giant gassy world must be very bright.
It's orbit double Pluto's which is quite a bit.
    One super-sized sun and two smaller suns
    slowly go around planet so lightly spun.

A year is half a millennium long since onset.
All three stars visible for one-fourth of a year.
How many appointments would residents forget
waiting to see where which suns would appear.
    The big sun is rising when
    two smaller ones are setting again.

How can a calendar keep things right?
Juggling three suns to figure out time?
Any beings could become uptight,
but the sunlight would be sublime.
    I'm sure any inhabitants could adapt.
    Might have their own cosmic app.

HD 131399Ab in Constellation Centaurus
has a very unwieldy, impersonal name.
This presents a challenge for us,
to give planet an approachable nickname.
    Are scientist protocols for naming under review?
    Temporarily called "The Planet" won't do.

This planet holds many mysteries before us.
A directly imaged exoplanet, not by dips in starlight--
a planet with triple stellar companions brings
astronomers and all Earthlings delight.
    Maybe name it Space Snail since it orbits so slowly.
    For millenniums it remains glowy, light-showy.

The Most Distant Galaxy

International team of astronomers proclaims
GN-z11 the most distant galaxy seen
in Ursa Major direction, with light
that left 13.4 billion years ago.
They believe universe is 13.8 billion years old
so GN-z11 gives us view of conditions
near the end of the Dark Ages of the universe
before first stars and quasars formed.

Hubble performed better than expected
but newer telescopes will be launched.
New discoveries found daily
expand what we think we know,
recognizing vast vacuum in what
might accurately be proven, even
with all our equipment, getting back
to creation could apply to just this universe.

As we poke among infinite space
finding billions of stars, galaxies,
beyond our access in multiverses
impossibly far away, dazzled by wonder
we should look at our speck of spectacular planet.
Alone or not in the cosmos, take care
of what we experience, responsibly,
enjoy the stelliferous era while we can.

Settling Other Worlds

Our time on Earth is finite
so we must find another place to thrive.
Look outward. That's definite.
The only way our species will survive.
        We may have the distinction
        of causing our own extinction.

So we must find another place to thrive.
Some other beings might be living there.
They might feel to remain alive,
Earthlings are not welcome to share.
        They might know of our record.
        Not feel we'd be in accord.

Look outward. That's definite.
The universe is expanding.
Getting harder to reach for granite.
Technology beyond our understanding.
        We may as well not pretend.
        We may be here until bitter end.

The only way our species will survive
could be to become a hybrid.
Join the cosmic community and live
as some cyborg, robot, holographic kid.
        Who is to say our kind is needed
        in favor of some being alien-seeded?

We may have the distinction
of making a dimensional shift,
or instantly demolished by radiation,
set molecularly cosmically adrift.
        Our consciousness may formlessly roam
        and not seek a physical home.

Of causing our own extinction,
pundits say its our responsibility,
to give planetary survival our attention
to enhance Gaia's sustainability.
        But the universe may have other plans
        for Earth's violent, contentious clans.

Landing on Mars

Earthlings send to Mars: orbiters, landers and probes
        leaving behind our space junk,
        equipment gone defunct,
adding to debris from other cosmic globes?

Lander Schiaparelli is the latest to crash.
        Two spacecraft roam the surface.
        Curiosity and Opportunity deface,
soon they'll join our other space trash.

They're seven successful robotic landings.
        Wind and dust hinder spacecraft inbound
        but orbiters still spin around
to broaden our Martian understandings.

Our mission is to find life elsewhere
        or a place we can migrate to someday.
        But maybe aliens will get in our way?
Maybe Martians don't want to share?

Perhaps other entities there might think
        we are coming to take over
        and they're hunkering under cover.
Perhaps we'd be mining, taking a Martian chink?

By the time we can reach there intact
        and we might need Mars for refuge
        from solar flares or nuclear deluge--
we may not be welcome, deterred in fact.

Mars is a potentially rich real estate
        an advanced race could terraform,
        find sustainable ways to transform.
Our technology might be perfected too late.

NASA's Mars Reconnaissance Orbiter records
        ill-fated missions, transmits back bad news.
        Other spacecraft seek other cosmic clues.
We'll try again when some agency affords.

But I wonder about any Martian consciousness.
        How many civilizations came there before?
        Are they willing to endure intrusion once more?
They might perceive doom with our success.

Martian Destiny?

Were' going to Mars
       to live there?
It is in our stars?
       In the air?
So when our Earth scars
       we can't bear
we will look afar?
       Will Mars care?

We'll bring modulars.
       Will need spare?
Underground dwellers–
       cave repair?
Now crepusculars.
       Should beware?
New vernaculars
       to declare?
Devise calendars
       to share?

We're raising the bars.
       We aware?
Become stellulars?
       We'd compare?
Use binoculars,
       new software?
Define particulars?
       Should we dare?

Star Beings

Are aliens coming bringing humanity hope?
I study perspectives on universal breeding.
11th Dimensional beings widen my scope.
Ancestors believed in Star Beings' seeding.
>   Now the universe is a holographic projection.
>   Dream Times, Akashic Records, The Cloud archive collection.

I study perspectives on universal breeding.
I think we are star stuff and have stellar assistance.
Open minds and best information we're heeding?
Organized groups, other aliens provide resistance?
>   I ponder new ways to celestially believe
>   and new possibilities to cosmically perceive.

11th Dimensional beings widen my scope
as I contemplate transmissions in Earthlings' behalf,
empowering grids, frequencies to help us cope,
bringing change to this Earth-based holograph.
>   Multidimensional beings suggest we're all connected.
>   We are not alone. Old concepts rejected.

Ancestors believed in Star Being's seeding,
gave Star Beings credit for bringing knowledge,
protection from extinctions, civilizations succeeding.
Oral traditions, rituals and art all acknowledge
>   visitations, various E.T. landings
>   broadening their understandings.

Now the universe is a holographic projection,
At least some scientists think this is so.
Who runs the projectors? For our protection?
How controlling? We don't know.
>   We provide digital data they could use
>   to help, hinder, infuse our muse.

Dream times, Akashic Records, The Cloud archive collection
of all experiences, ideas- all universal existence
recorded, accessible, for multidimensional selection.
How is information used and by whom, for instance
>   can determine our extermination or paradise.
>   We can only hope cosmic planners are wise.

Why Would E.T.'s Come Here?

Are we their cosmic experiment?
They have to keep track of us?
They need to intervene per agreement
because we cause a galactic fuss?
       Do they come to help or control?
       Do they want resources or to patrol?

They have to keep track of us
because we are not evolving according to plan?
Our breaches are incredulous
and they need to do what they can?
       Some say we have free will,
       but they'll find a way to enter still.

They need to intervene per agreement,
if we mismanage our universal position.
We've caused some colossal disagreement,
putting the Milky Way in perilous condition.
       Some say misuse of nuclear power,
       makes this galaxy's aliens cower.

Because we cause a galactic fuss
and the earthly powers in charge
have caused such a dysfunctional ruckus,
the alien contact must enlarge.
       Not just alien abductions, but troops on the ground.
       Then Earth can become an alien compound.

Do they come to help or control?
Will they enslave us or befuddle our minds?
Obliterate the species, set a new protocol?
I doubt they will cuddle their finds.
       Let's be honest, no nonsense.
       Earthlings are a cosmic nuisance.

Do they want resources or to patrol?
We have many treasures for their coffers.
Do they have their own needs, perhaps a soul
to fulfill here or will they explore other offers?
       They might not even want to stay,
       take what they want and go away.

What is the Universe Made Of?

What the universe is made of remains a mystery.
Scientists discover so such complexity
and no answers for dark matter and dark energy.

The inadequate Standard Model theory
shifted to incomplete Supersymmetry.
They are still searching for Susy.

There is so much more to learn
as they smash particles at CERN
causing some grave concern.

Is dark matter cold or hot?
We just know we have a lot
putting physicists on the spot.

They look for wimps and axions,
even think there are Hooperons
to join the possible Higgs Bosons.

All these particles zoom through us.
Unseen without light to guide us.
Dark matter and energy surround us.

I see all the complicated math and my mind swirls.
But math into theory not often unfurls.
The universe continues to conceal its pearls.

They talk about science and spirituality
working together to explain reality.
Both views still face unknowns actually.

There may be multiverses and dimensions
demanding deep thinkers' attentions.
Not yet with any inventions.

As for me , I accept my ineptitude
with a curious, open attitude
and a sense of gratitude.

End of Space/Time

This universe could end in trillions of years,
not in Big Crunch, Big Rip, but Big Freeze,
unless a Phase Transition, bubble universe appears
or space fabric poked by black holes catastrophes.
Until all the stars blink out
we have lots to think about.

Not in Big Crunch, Big Rip, but Big Freeze
this universe expands darkly getting colder.
We know of no Prime Creator to appease
we just go on getting expanded and older.
This is the current scientific abstraction,
so enjoy this warmer, brighter attraction.

Unless a Phase Transition bubble universe appears
or an asteroid hits Earth or sun fries us,
to end consciousness of these instinctual fears,
we deal with what certainty denies us.
Perhaps we have it all wrong
and another future comes along.

Or space fabric poked by black hole catastrophes
until it ceases gorging space exports.
Then cold, darkness, extinction of any entities,
even end of infinitesimal primordial orts.
But that's projected end of this universe,
what about gap left in the multiverse?

Until all the stars blink out
and there is no more heat or light,
all connections link out
with no one to know our plight,
we could adapt a less fatal attitude
and live this life speck with gratitude.

We have lots to think about
and many things we want to do,
actions to go to the brink about
before this sentience session is through.
Perhaps in other dimensions
beings face different comprehensions?

The Unified Field

The unified field contains us all, all souls, all time, all space, all matter.
What affects one, affects One.   Sara Wiseman

What expansiveness and turbulence within the unified field!
Impossible to know and comprehend its vast dominion.
Is this One for what this universe can yield?
Are there One's in the cosmos of differing opinion?
> Macro, micro, megalo-- all affect each entity.
> Makes one ponder one's responsibility.

Impossible to know and comprehend its dominion.
We blast onto the scene, once a supernova.
As an Earthling we hope to find a guiding companion,
after a sperm connects among ova.
> Energy and consciousness all over the realm.
> Some experiences tend to overwhelm.

Is this One for what this universe can yield?
Are their other organizing principles elsewhere
in other dimensions, universes–what forces do they wield?
If we breakthrough, they might not want us there.
> Are we on a disc, brane or bubble?
> Whatever, we cause a bit of trouble.

Are there Ones in the cosmos of differing opinion
on how One's elements should evolve?
Do they divvy out to committees of minions,
ways their problems can resolve?
> We can certainly see we are not alone.
> Are we All a stellar cosmic clone?

Macro, micro, megalo–all affect each entity.
Under control? Chaos? Unknown protocol?
Maybe varying fields struggle within this unity?
Sometimes it seems its just a free-for-all.
> How puzzling for the new arrival,
> wondering about long-term survival.

Makes one ponder one's responsibility
within this web, wave, misty net.
We can do our best to our ability,
to live with love, not regret.
> Can we ever do enough
> to fulfill our role as star stuff?

Clouds: Haiku Variations

Traditional...

On spring horizon
conifers scratch gray-bottomed
rain-itchy, storm clouds.

Contemporary...

spring horizon
conifers scratch bottoms
of storm clouds

Lune-words...

Playful angels roll
halos on bumpy dark clouds
dance hip-hop thunderously.

Lune-syllables...

Blue Earth seen from space
mapped with clouds
view full Earth first time.

Hay (na) ku...

rainbows
frown down
smile at sky

Katauta...

What does spring look like?
Can you tell when it has come?
I am waiting–long.

color fades in fog
rain stipples leaves with clear daubs
dew dapples diamonds.

Crystaline...

Sharp-edged contrails rip the sky, puncture clouds.
They blur into gauzy scars.

Tweeku...

Sunset's
palette painted by
angels.

Sunrise
spills angels' paint
buckets.

Cinqku...

Fairies
vacation
on cloudy lofts,
sneeze pollution
back to earth acid rain.

American Sentence...

Clouds recycle elements for cycle of life–don't clog the process.

Miku...

Rascal angels
tickle clouds
tinkle rain.

Choka...

Angels peek-a-boo
behind billowy, buffed clouds.
GPS flight assignments
zoom destinations–
invisibly enter realm
release through their cloud cover.

Tanka...

Cloud inhabitants
are multi-dimensional.
Unseen they exist.
Many dimensions dream
in these clouds of unknowing.

Dodoitsu

Why is cloud 9 so amazing?
What is wrong with cloud 8? Ten?
Bright spot in every dark cloud?
Sky dark with war clouds, peace clears?
Will dark clouds light in starry night?

Guyku...

Hi, I'm Earth's clouds.
Part of celestial crowds
becoming lethal shrouds?

Naga-Uta...

Clouds nourish spirit
more than I can intuit.
Clouds protect us from void,
radiation to avoid.
Clouds can beautify
shapes and colors of our sky.
Clouds are dream-keepers,
diligent cosmic sweepers.

Cinquo...

Clouds

Wet
sponge
sop up seas
then squeeze to soak
us.

Lanterne...

Raindrops

Sky
spits, sprays
gathers to
bend so rainbows
arc.

Kimo...

Clouds are Gaia's clinging companions,
sky-lovers yet touching moist ground,
conversing with sight, sound.

Acknowlegments

Other Poetry Books by Linda Varsell Smith

Cinqueries: A Cluster of Cinquos and Lanterns
Fibs and Other Truths
Black Stars on a White Sky
Poems That Count
Poems That Count Too.
Winging-It New and Selected Poems
Red Cape Capers: Playful Backyard Meditations
Star Stuff: A Soul- Splinter Experiences the Cosmos
Light-Headed: A Soul-Splinter Experiences Light
Sparks: A Soul-Splinter Experiences Earth

Chapbooks

Being Cosmic
Intra-space Chronicles
Light-Headed
Red Cape Capers

On-Line Web-site Books:
Free Access@ www.rainbowcommunications.org

Syllable of Velvet
Word-Playful
Poetluck

Anthologies

The Second Genesis
Branches
Poetic License
Poetic License 2015
Jubillee
The Eloquent Umbrella

Twelve Novels in the Rainbow Chronicle Series.

www.ingramcontent.com/pod-product-compliance
Lightning Source LLC
Chambersburg PA
CBHW030916090426
42737CB00007B/216